THE CONSULTING DATA OBSESSIVE

Solving the Mystery of Being Data Rich ... and Information Poor

J. BRIAN FARISH

First edition 2021

ISBN 978-1-7379452-0-8 (paperback)
ISBN 978-1-7379452-1-5 (ebook)

www.theconsultingdataobsessive.com

Publisher: Liberty OPS, LLC

CONTENTS

ILLUSTRATIONS

FOREWORD

By Dr. Terry Halpin

I first met Brian and his lovely wife Linda many years ago in the USA at an industrial conference focused on information modelling and database design. On a personal level, I found Brian to be open, honest, and genuinely warm and gentlemanly in the best Texan tradition.

On a professional level, I was impressed with Brian's understanding of the practical advantages of first working with business experts to understand their information requirements and then conceptualize an information model in language easily understood by them, before exploiting the conceptual information model to facilitate the design of an actual implementation such as a relational database design. His passion and commitment to this modelling approach has remained undiminished in his long and successful career in industry.

Brian has worked for many years as a principal consultant and chief information architect for a wide variety of prestigious companies. His industrial experience in working both individually and especially in teams has given him a deep understanding of the practicalities and realities of working in complex IT environments, and what is needed to improve the quality of the end product.

In this book, Brian clearly communicates many of the lessons acquired from his practical experience. His writing style is easy to follow, and his engaging story telling reads more like an interesting novel than a technical document.

Sprinkled throughout the text are several well-chosen quotes to convey salient points, as well as illuminating diagrams to summarize clearly the important ideas.

The practical issues discussed in this book are especially relevant to any practitioner who wishes to convince management of the benefits of first establishing a clear view of the information requirements from the business experts and then specifying an information model using concepts easily understood and validated by them, before using that information model to develop the data designs used in the actual implementations.

This approach enhances the likelihood of developing information systems that are not only error-free, but easier to modify as the business needs change, and easier to integrate with other existing systems as needed.

ACKNOWLEDGMENTS

When I finished the first draft of this book, I asked for some help spreading the word, and **Dr. Terry Halpin** graciously asked to see a copy of the book after it was published. Since Terry's work has had a significant impact on how I view information and data, I rushed him a copy. I was honored when he provided feedback, and his observations made this a better book. His contributions to information architecture are exceeded only by his grace and generosity. I am grateful for every chance I've had to spend time with him and his contributions to my professional development.

This book probably would never have happened without the direct influence and encouragement of my good friend **Chris Young**. He is a brilliant mind, generous soul, creative spirit, gifted leader, and my life has been blessed by his presence.

The single most significant influence on my professional career was my association with **Gary Schuldt**. Gary challenged me to think and look for the "meta" in the scenarios we faced in his classes and working together on projects. I am incredibly grateful for the time he invested, and I try to "pay it forward" whenever I can.

I encountered the **Kallman family** over 25 years ago and have been blessed by the acquaintance beyond words. **Dan** is an inspirational leader, and **Andy** is a gifted thought leader and agent of change. **Ted** combined those qualities with a mischievous, warped sense of humor that made working with him a blessing and truly memorable.

Everyone experiences good and bad projects, but I had the opportunity to lead a team in setting up a Master Data Management environment in my first experience as a Chief Data Officer. I sincerely hope that everyone gets the chance to be a part of a professional, high-performing team such as that one at least once in their career. **Vikram Parvathaneni** and **Randy Nguyen** are two of the brightest and most effective I/T professionals with whom it has ever been my honor to work, and I look forward to watching them grow and excel professionally.

God blessed me with an older brother who has been a mentor, sounding board and friend my whole professional career. When I needed a non-technical perspective on this book, **Harvey** happily pitched in and was predictably effective in helping me make this work better. Thank you, Harvey.

Saving the best for last, I wish to thank **my wife, Linda,** for being my best friend on this journey. I could not have asked for a better match in a battle of wills, a more tender heart for trying times, or a more devoted fur-baby parent for all of the critters with which we have been blessed. Stealing a song lyric, "I love you more today than yesterday… but not as much as tomorrow."

PREFACE

> **"It is a capital mistake to theorize before one has data. Insensibly one begins to twist facts to suit theories, instead of theories to suit facts."**
> - Sir Arthur Conan Doyle, Sherlock Holmes

FIGURE 1 - SHERLOCK HOLMES ON DATA

A discussion of data and the information it represents is surprisingly complicated. The interchangeable way many people use the terms confuses and complicates the discussion about how to proceed. This book attempts to clarify misunderstandings around information and data and lay out a path to achieving a genuinely information-driven approach to automating a modern business enterprise.

But here are four key ideas that you should take away from this book:

1-2-3-4 Summary

1. If you only take **one** thing away from this book, I hope it is an understanding of how important it is to obtain precise business language descriptions. You should gather them early and for every single term in your business domain and especially every single term referring to a data element.
2. We describe **two** different approaches to becoming an information-driven enterprise. To answer the question, "Well, what would you do if completely empowered?" I present the "greenfield" or ideal approach in the Baker of Baker Street storyline and the "Metamorphosis" section. To describe a more incremental approach appropriate for large, complex enterprises, I describe some strategies in the Mycroft Industries storyline and the "Incremental Improvement" section.
3. There are **three** primary functions to think about in trying to shift any organization in a new direction.
   1. **Sell**ing the idea
   2. **Plan**ning the work
   3. **Do**ing the work
4. There are **four** levels of planning to break down any effort effectively, and they have a definite parent-child relationship:
   1. Vision – know where you are going
   2. Strategies – understand how you plan to get there
   3. People/Projects – for change management, people and influence are the priority; for delivery management, projects help compartmentalize the effort into manageable chunks.
   4. Tasks – "To do" list work to be accomplished

Context

During four decades of work in information technologies and nearly three decades focusing primarily on data integration and information quality, a few key lessons stand out that need to be shared here. But the most important lesson learned is that explaining what is needed is relatively simple. However, explaining why it is required and how to do it effectively in clear enough language to motivate harried executives and stressed-out staff to take action is less straightforward.

With that in mind, this book attempts to cover the major activities involved in implementing enterprise information (selling the vision, planning how to accomplish the vision, and doing the work to achieve the vision) using two different approaches, story-telling and explanation. This two-pronged approach is not new, and it has been employed masterfully by others, so there is a pretty high standard to be met.

The hope is that the explanatory portion will provide some helpful reference material and tools to jump-start further study in the subject. The story-telling section aims to be more conversational and share various practical ideas and perspectives.

Additionally, by detailing some common challenges for this kind of work, it is hoped that data architects in "the heat of battle" can receive encouragement that their struggles are not unique.

The fundamental message of this work is the need for precise communication between:

- The business and I/T [language of business to language of technology]
- I/T and I/T(now) [across development teams and technologies]

- I/T(local) and I/T(remote) [across geographies, cultures, and languages
- I/T(current) and I/T(future) [across time]

For this to happen, we need clear, exhaustive, unambiguous business language definitions to be captured for all business terms of significance, and especially for business terms represented by data elements. **This process of capturing clear definitions for data elements creates the *bridge* between *business semantics* [the information the business needs] and *technical syntax* [the data that I/T manages to represent the information].**

The more time and effort a project team invests in defining the vocabulary of the scope of their project up front, the smoother <u>everything</u> will proceed after that.

Humans developed language to get an idea from one person's head into another person's head. To do that, both parties must have a shared understanding of what each word means. When there is a misunderstanding about what the words mean, there is a communication breakdown, sometimes with disastrous results.

We sometimes forget that computers do the same thing as language; however, computers add speed, consistency, computation, persistent storage, and asynchronous access to the mix. But fundamentally, the goal is the same: human-to-human communication.

The development of artificial intelligence [AI] changed things up just a bit. However, since initial implementations of AI are an extension of the humans who created them, the pattern still applies. As AI evolves to the point of not communicating with humans anymore but instead optimizes communications with other AI instances, humans will have to derive semantic meaning from observation of cause-and-effect scenarios. But as long as there is a communication link between the AI and human beings (e.g., humans interpreting output from AI), there must be solid semantics.

The principles and techniques to achieve better information will be presented and demonstrated in story form and a more formal presentation. The hope is that explaining the principles may plant the concepts, and then seeing the principles in context and engaging a different part of the brain might reinforce them.

What to Expect

A good idea must be sold in multiple ways, multiple times, and at various levels of detail to become a reality. People with different priorities, vocabularies, skill sets, and motivations make up the community that will make the idea a reality. Executive leadership can't simply legislate the changes outlined in this work successfully. Nor will they be accomplished purely as a grassroots effort from the bottom up because the pace of modern business, conflicting agendas, and immediate (perceived) priorities will eventually swamp the strategic thinking and activities necessary to move an initiative forward. There is a worn cliché that admonishes, "Don't try to boil the ocean." Still, for this kind of effort to succeed, all participants must have their information-awareness temperature raised at whatever pace possible.

As has been mentioned in passing, every project or initiative in large organizations must complete three major activity sets to succeed:

- **Selling** the Vision
- **Planning** how to accomplish the Vision
- **Doing** the work necessary to achieve the Vision

From experience, the process of driving change at most enterprises involves **selling** the executives (Covered in the "Why? [Sell it]" section), **planning** the strategies to move forward (Covered in the "Approaches [Plan it]" section), and **delivering** (Covered in the "Do it" section) the desired results.

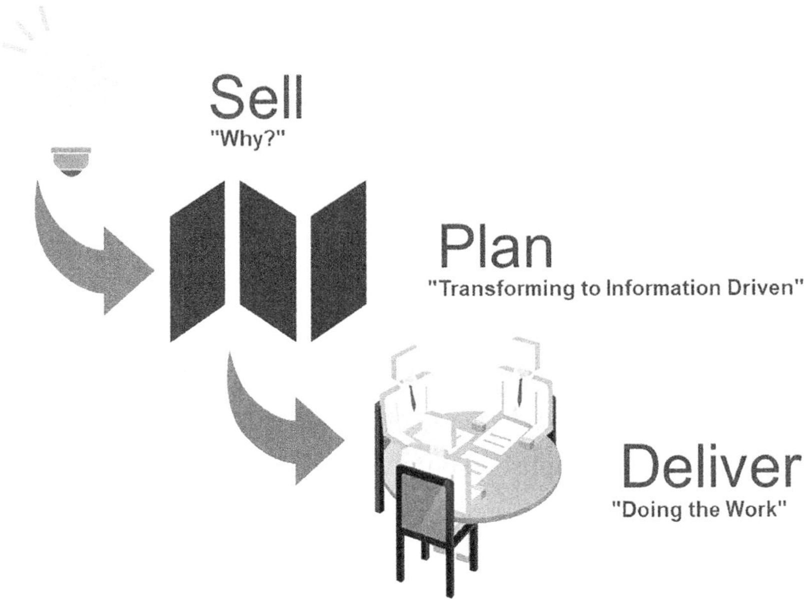

FIGURE 2 - SELL, PLAN, DELIVER

Sell it

The "**Why**? [Sell it]" section focuses on selling the need and benefits of Conceptual Information Architecture to executive-level leadership. It makes a case for funding and supporting the shift from an application/systems and process-driven enterprise to an Information-driven Enterprise. Executives are less concerned with the "how" concerns and more driven by return-on-investment. They are focused strategically on positioning the enterprise to harvest any short-term profits and benefits from current operations. However, executive leaders are also trying to enable the enterprise to adapt to changing business constraints, take advantage of future opportunities, and rapidly adopt emerging technologies.

It is the job of executive leadership to formulate a **Vision** for the future worded clearly enough to inform and guide the **Strategies** pursued in driving the enterprise toward that Vision. There are differing opinions on how specific and lengthy an overall vision statement for an enterprise should be. However, you must explicitly word the vision statement for handling the enterprise's data needs to include essential information and provide a reality check for old thinking regarding technology. (e.g., "In the future, ExWhyZee, LLC shall implement technology as equal-partner cooperation between business and I/T. Business shall provide resources to specify and explain information requirements, and I/T shall design and implement systems in such a way that the data captured to meet those information requirements is clearly understood and accurately, securely, and flexibly stored in such a way as to make it accessible to authorized parties.").

Plan it

The "**Approaches [Plan it]**" section focuses on the **executives, managers, and architects** that create the **Strategies** to make the Vision a reality.

Two different strategic approaches are offered for consideration and as thought starters. The first ("Metamorphosis") is an "ideal" transformation effort. While business realities make it unlikely that any modern enterprise of significant size will follow it line-by-line, it does serve to describe an ideal goal and provide a baseline. New businesses could also organize things in alignment with the "Metamorphosis" pattern and position themselves to dominate their market as they grow and develop a significant informational advantage over their competition.

Architecting Requirements vs. Designing Solutions

One of the themes repeated throughout this work is that the goal is to architect information requirements before designing data solutions. Understanding the distinction between these two activities has proven to be one of the biggest challenges for I/T resources. As technologists, our training and focus have been on taking ideas and transforming them into technology-enabled solutions. However, it is vital to stop "thinking ahead" to the ultimate technological design and imposing technical constraints into what is supposed to be a purely business-needs-driven document. A technically agnostic map is an architecture of what the business needs to know (the conceptual information requirements) rather than a design of how to provide it using a particular technology. Being technically agnostic ensures that no details of the business requirement get "dropped on the floor" because they are inconvenient for the technology du jour.

Do it

The "**Do it**" section shares some of the **tools** necessary to parse plain business language and deliver an architected model of the information requirements of the business. This information requirements model can serve to inform future logical design efforts. The non-technology-specific nature of the information model is a critical feature. The information model should only change over time as business strategies and new regulatory requirements become factors in collecting and processing information.

The Information Renaissance Professional

Being an effective information architecture consultant requires some level of skill in:

- semantics
- information modeling (conceptual)
- data modeling (logical)
- database modeling (physical)
- enterprise architecture
- presentation
- technical evangelism
- project management
- database design
- change management
- meeting facilitation
- conflict resolution
- and on and on

While these topics are touched upon here, far better resources are available for deep dives on them. Therefore, the focus of this discussion will be effectively combining these skills. The goal is to enable companies to position themselves to know what they need to know when they need to know it and be prepared to deal with new information requirements and new technologies as they encounter them.

The first of the three critical activity sets that we will discuss at length is the "Why?" or "Sell it" activity set. The goal is to equip the reader with tools to inform and persuade colleagues of the necessity and benefits of an information-centric approach to systems and data.

WHY?
[Sell it]

"More data was generated in the last two years than in the **entire human history** before that."[3]

"...99.5% of collected data never gets used or analyzed."[3]

"Less than 50% of the structured data collected from IoT is used in decision making." [3]

A recent survey[5] of 23,000 data professionals estimated that data professionals spend around 23% of their time cleaning data. While that does not rise to the apocryphal 80% level that many have been guilty of quoting without checking the source, it still adds up to an entire day out of each workweek on average that data professionals spend doing nothing but cleaning up bad data. This inefficiency is a shameful state to have reached in the evolution of "information" systems at this late date. Progressive-thinking leaders need to be asking themselves, "Is this the way I want my data scientists to have to be spending their time?"

After seventy years of analysis, architecture, deep thought, and trial-and-error, why has the I/T landscape in so many enterprises and the global environment evolved into such a scattered collection of siloed data systems that struggle so mightily to connect and create meaningful information? Why does Fear, Uncertainty, and Doubt [FUD] regarding data quality and data security still haunt executive leadership?

Fundamentally, the issue is that most of the effort and focus has been on optimizing the technologies involved while paying little attention to the quality of the "raw material" (the data) created and consumed. These misplaced priorities have caused the end-product (the information) to be sub-optimal when the business uses it.

> **Technological progress has merely provided us with more efficient means for going backwards.**
> – Aldous Huxley

FIGURE 3 - RACING TO THE REAR

Imagine a hypothetical scenario where the construction industry focused on the rapid development of newer, faster tools and conveyances of raw materials while never researching and establishing quality standards and governance for the materials used in the impressive architectural wonders around us. Then, when the bridges began to collapse, it is a safe bet that the cry would not be that "We need better tools!", "We need better railroads and trucks to transport the materials!", or "Build faster!". No, we know absolutely that the industry would do a root-cause analysis, identify inferior materials, and develop processes to prevent such a thing from ever happening again.

If "Data is the new oil" or "Data is the new gold"[13], why is it so far-fetched and unreasonable that we require the same care and governance processes for our data as for our finances? Is it merely the less "tangible" nature of data that makes it so hard to achieve "buy-in" for disciplined architecture and governance?

There is a lot of talk about "data-driven organizations." But the reality is that we have a tsunami of data in most organizations but a parched field as far as quality information is concerned, a "target-rich" set of information opportunities missed by systems firing blanks. So it is time to discuss the realities of the opportunity, the challenges, some paths forward, and the mechanics of making things better.

> **The reasonable man adapts himself to the world; the unreasonable one persists in trying to adapt the world to himself. Therefore all progress depends on the unreasonable man.**
>
> - George Bernard Shaw, Man and Superman, 1903

FIGURE 4 - UNREASONABLE MAN

Information vs. Data

For this discussion, "information" refers to what an enterprise wants or needs to know, and "data" refers to how I/T chooses to encode or represent that information. Information is driven by semantics (the meaning), and data is constrained by syntax (the storage pattern). Information is a requirement, and data are used within an implementation to fulfill a requirement. They are not the same thing despite the terms being used interchangeably throughout the I/T industry. This discussion focuses on the need to formally derive a Conceptual Information Model (CIM) for the business, describing the landscape of information desired by the company and some techniques and approaches to making that happen.

Expanded Information Capabilities

As the world tries to move toward a seamlessly integrated digital marketplace and maximize the potential of machine learning, artificial intelligence, and predictive analytics, getting systems to communicate effectively in a reasonable amount of time remains a persistent challenge.

Insights derived from these efforts are only as valid as the quality of the data used to create them and the clarity of the shared understanding of the meaning of the data. Therein lies the root of the problem.

A Legacy of Technical Debt

A helpful term that has become widely used in industry is "Technical Debt," and as used here, "*... reflects the implied cost of additional rework caused by choosing an easy (limited) solution now instead of using a better approach that would take longer.*" [2]

Most of the current applications were created as functionally siloed point solutions and evolved organically via rushed development processes, emphasizing specific business processes and user-interface-driven priorities without considering integrating into a broader information universe.

The result is a "data universe" (see earlier distinction re: "data" vs. "information") composed of hundreds of functionally specific data silos that are unable to "talk" to each other without a significant effort on the part of the potential information consumers.

Root Cause

Business/IT Disconnect

If the ladder is not leaning against the right wall, every step we take just gets us to the wrong place faster.

- Stephen Covey

FIGURE 5 - WRONG DIRECTION

The reasons that I/T implements ill-defined systems are diverse. However, a major contributing factor is that the content and quality of the information captured should be the priority of the **business**. Still, traditionally, the business side of the enterprise defers to I/T to produce a solution. They may toss off a few notes about desired features and functionality, but then they will sit back and wait for something to be delivered. I/T is hesitant to ask clarifying questions that may complicate the requirements and, therefore, delay the roll-out of the systems they are building or implementing. So, assumptions are made that get baked into the architecture of the system. By the time the testers or end users discover the erroneous assumptions, a significant code base typically exists, transforming the incorrect assumptions into "bugs" and inaccurate data. The cost of fixing the situation increases ten-fold with every development phase (requirements, design, development, testing, production) or sprint that passes before the error presents itself.

The ERP Shortcut Myth

One aspect of the "root cause" frequently encountered is the assertion that "Oh, we purchased YahdeeYahdee ERP system, so we just use the definitions they provide." Upon further investigation, it is not unusual for the analysts to discover that either the "descriptions" are a restatement of the variable's name or else so terse and ambiguously worded as to constrain nothing and render deriving data quality edits based upon the description virtually impossible. This situation should not be a surprise to anyone who thinks about it for a bit. These ERP vendors are trying to create a solution to implement broadly across many different industries and business models; therefore, the attribute definitions must remain "loose" to accommodate various business models. However, that very "looseness," if not "tightened up" for an organization's specific business processes and information needs, leads to poorly edited and largely ungoverned data, unfit for analytics and integrations without significant rework.

The "Agile Does not Need This" Myth

The Agile methodology does not readily deal with these issues because implementing flawed assumptions in small chunks still means that errors are baked into the codebase. Agile does a fantastic job of evolving business and system processes and user interfaces. The erroneous underlying information content assumptions we are focusing on are just as detrimental to an Agile development team as they were to traditional "waterfall" projects.

The promise of "refactoring" tools to mitigate the disruption caused by the late-stage discovery of erroneous data assumptions has been made for the last twenty years. Still, it is yet to be widely implemented successfully. When it becomes widely available, "evolving" data and code to make up for missed information requirements will be less costly and detrimental; however, it remains that the most cost-effective time to catch a requirement is before the design and coding begin. Additionally, the issue of end-point consumers (interface developers, data scientists, analysts, etc.) needing clear definitions to consume, analyze and govern the data appropriately remains unaddressed.

To be clear, the approach we are encouraging will position Agile teams for successful outcomes and enterprises for strategic information capabilities.

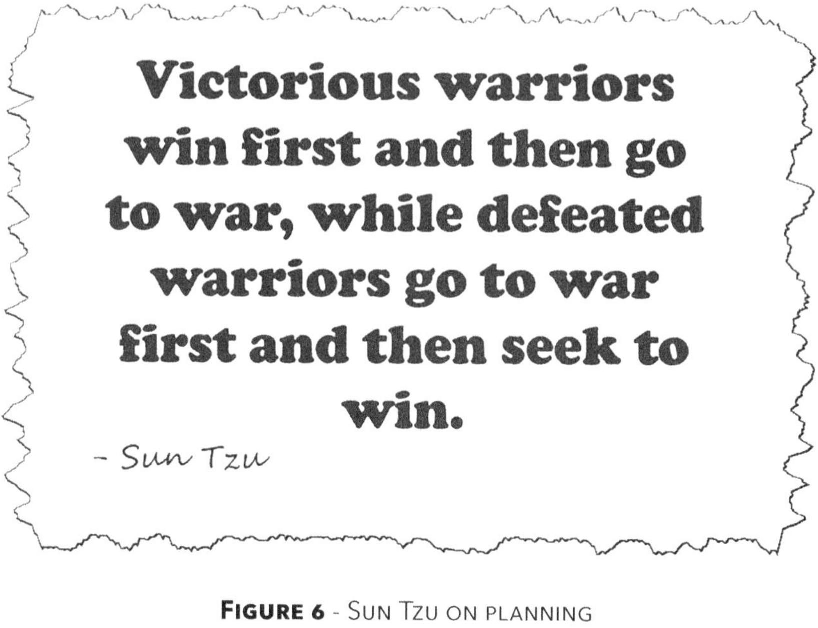

FIGURE 6 - SUN TZU ON PLANNING

The "Silver Bullet Technology" Myth

> **It will take you less time and effort to do a thing the difficult way than it will to buy, try and discard all the shortcuts.**
> - Seth Godin

FIGURE 7 - SILVER BULLETS COST MORE THAN THEIR PURCHASE PRICE

One of the biggest hurdles to be overcome in selling conceptual information architecture to I/T resources and enterprises, in general, is the frustrating assumption that if an information problem exists, it's just because I/T hasn't purchased the correct software yet.

Compounding this bias is an entire multi-billion-dollar technology industry paying salespeople to go out and focus on "what can sell." But, unfortunately, better information definitions and better information governance processes are sufficiently dull, uninspiring, and complicated enough to make these high-pressure salespeople roll their eyes and quickly begin to work on their next presentation slide.

The real solution to reliable enterprise information is not a solution that enterprises can purchase. Instead, it is a fundamental shift in organizational priorities and perspectives on technology enablement within the enterprise.

The REAL "Silver Bullet"

The process of distilling clear business definitions for all significant information elements at the enterprise level yields benefits in several ways. First, it increases the quality of any data designs based on them. Second, it identifies "unknowns" (questions) and details about the business, business processes, and regulatory requirements that allow for a better ultimate design and will pay off ten-fold in avoided rework and information quality.

The Importance of Semantics

This book is not primarily about semantics but about modeling "meaning" versus "design." Hence, it is helpful for us to establish why semantics matter to Information Technology (I/T) projects.

> **Without knowing the force of words, it is impossible to know human beings.**
> - *Confucius, Analects, (~500 B.C.)*

FIGURE 8 - WORDS

While the importance of precise semantics has been recognized for decades (e.g., phonetic alphabet, corporate business glossaries, etc.), for some reason, the adoption of semantics as a priority has been slow to catch on in most I/T organizations and particularly at the project level.

Why are I/T projects so resistant to semantic clarity?

It is easy these days to get a positive reaction from senior executives when mentioning the need to foster "data-driven enterprises." Talk about predictive analytics, machine learning, artificial intelligence, data science, blockchain enablement, etc., and they will look like bobblehead dolls on the dashboard of a car going over a railroad track. Vendors and pundits selling technology-based solutions gloss over the realities of what is required and the degree to which most organizations would have to change to implement such a philosophy. There is not currently a purely technological solution to this need. Still, you would never know this from most software pitches because none address the fundamental "change management" required within leadership and across the entire organization.

The problem is that the distinction between syntax (how the data is structured) and semantics (the information the data represents) is not widely understood and accepted by I/T resources or business leadership.

The two worlds operate with a high degree of independence from each other. Executive (Business) Leadership crafts Vision statements and makes pronouncements about broad strategies. The I/T organizations busily acquire new technologies and implement systems vaguely informed and loosely guided by the controlling Vision. The two environments and perspectives speak different languages and have distinctly different priorities.

The obvious nature of the value of definitions paradoxically leads to them being de-prioritized by executives and developers. They assume that definitions exist *somewhere*. Without deep reflection and experience, it is just too easy to toss off statements like "Well, everyone knows what an order is..." or "Oh, we have the definitions provided by SAP" and rush to the next meeting. As a result, definitions get lumped in with "documentation" and are considered anathema by most developers.

Communication Breakdown

One of the challenges is aligning the tactical operational activities and priorities with the strategic requirements of the business. For example, the tactical operational activities are the I/T resources implementing systems, whereas the strategic requirements are the vision and strategies of executive leadership. Ted and Andy Kallman outline this disconnect in their book[1], describing a "Language of Leadership" employed by executives to express their vision. At the same time, managers and staff use a "Language of Management" describing day-to-day actions used to implement the vision. The problems occur when the two languages are not in alignment.

A similar breakdown occurs in I/T, but on top of shifting from "Language of Leadership" to "Language of Management," an added fork of confusion is caused by adding a "Syntax of Technology."

Each different technical implementation (RDBMS, Hadoop, flat files, OODBMS, etc.) will have a different applicable "Syntax of Technology," which comes to bear in the Logical (first design) layer of the design hierarchy. At the logical level of design, constraints of the technology chosen by the I/T resources begin to weigh on the information requirements gathered in the interviews with the business.

The most disastrous implementations result from accepting vague conceptual requirements and just "jumping" straight into a logical design of a solution. Unfortunately, this is how a large percentage of the implementations of systems happen. Often justified as following a philosophy of "fail fast," the assumption is that Agile teams readily address all issues by iterating over the requirements with ever-refined technical implementation. The problem is that getting the underlying data structures wrong is like laying a crooked foundation and is not as easily fixed as getting a process wrong or a less-than-optimal user interface. The resulting differences between what the teams build and what is needed or desired manifest themselves as "bugs" and "burndown list" items and are incredibly and exponentially more expensive the later in the implementation cycle they are discovered. And if the developers and testers don't find them until after the system goes "live," the expense can be monumental and potentially catastrophic.

"You get what you measure."

Another challenge is that I/T projects rarely have a validated, approved data dictionary for in-scope manipulated data elements as one of their listed deliverables. But, again, this goes back to just a fundamental lack of awareness of the critical value of definitions.

This lack of accountability for definitions is typical because the business does not get involved in detailed project planning for the I/T projects. Therefore, the business has no voice in setting priorities and deliverables. The need is not glaringly apparent until months or years later when they try to do something with the data generated by the resulting systems. This lack of semantic clarity limits the usefulness of the data even within the specific siloed use case. However, it is even more damaging when the potential value of the data extends across the enterprise. The level of effort and potential for error increases exponentially with each disparate ill-defined data set included in each universe of investigation.

From experience, if even one of two given systems in an integration project has adequate definitions for the data to be shared, the process can move forward much more rapidly. In addition, having one of the data sets defined as a baseline gives that partner leverage in negotiating the transformations required to align with the other system in the integration.

Without explicit metadata (semantic description-related) milestones and gating checkpoints for information requirements, projects will understandably prioritize the deliverables and metrics that determine their perceived success.

"Speed trumps everything"

In the ever-increasingly competitive global marketplace, businesses pressure executives to deliver more, faster, and cheaper.

A large, incredibly complex international enterprise that had mainly grown via acquisition was trying to implement a "quote-to-cash" full-lifecycle dashboard bringing together multiple ERP systems into an integrated knowledge base. In the middle of it, one of the senior executives announced to the entire company that "Speed trumps everything," and suddenly, anything that did not shorten the software delivery timeline was deemed wasteful and of lower priority. "Speed trumps everything" accompanied by smug, patronizing smiles became the trump-card auto-response to any questions about data element clarity.

If speed indeed does trump everything, why do we have brakes and steering wheels on cars? Why aren't we just making the engines (or batteries/motors) bigger and bigger and focusing on traction? Now a reasonable person might say that the quote is being taken out of context. However, that is the problem with pithy glamour quotes. They can over-simplify complex topics to the point of absurdity. Agenda-driven individuals then abuse them to cover a multitude of sins, and this one was repeatedly abused in multiple project meetings after being uttered as executive guidance.

Albert Einstein reportedly once said, "The best design is the simplest one that works." [emphasis mine]

Consider:

- Can a system that moves data around and performs computations blazingly fast that leads the business to flawed or plain wrong conclusions be said to **work**?
- Suppose an enterprise has information needs that are going unfulfilled because they have a dozen or so functionally siloed applications that cannot effectively share roughly comparable data to create end-to-end visibility. Can those systems be said to **work** from an enterprise perspective?
- If an enterprise must spend person-months of effort on creating interfaces between internal systems to share data, can those systems be said to **work** effectively?
- If an enterprise must spend person-years of effort to onboard external business partners because of poor documentation of their internal systems, can those systems be said to **work** efficiently?

Technology-focus of I/T Organizations

At the heart of this struggle is the fundamental truth that I/T organizations are technology providers first and businesspeople second (if at all, truth be told). There is typically a level of hubris in most I/T leadership that they know the business well enough not to need to consult the business experts for their information requirements. Since I/T leadership usually gets assessed on how quickly they can implement new systems, they view any process steps slowing down the delivery of what *appears* to be a functioning system as distractions. After all, many data issues only become apparent weeks or months later, so their repair can be passed off simply as enhancements. Since information quality is fundamentally a business priority, the business must be more assertive and engaged in providing information requirements. The business leadership has to champion information quality initiatives and governance.

The challenge to maintaining executive-level support for Conceptual Information Modeling comes when information experts outline the steps required to implement information-quality policies and procedures. Just as most people favor weight loss until they hear what is necessary to achieve it, most executives want an easy, cheap, fast, and effective path to the information promised land.

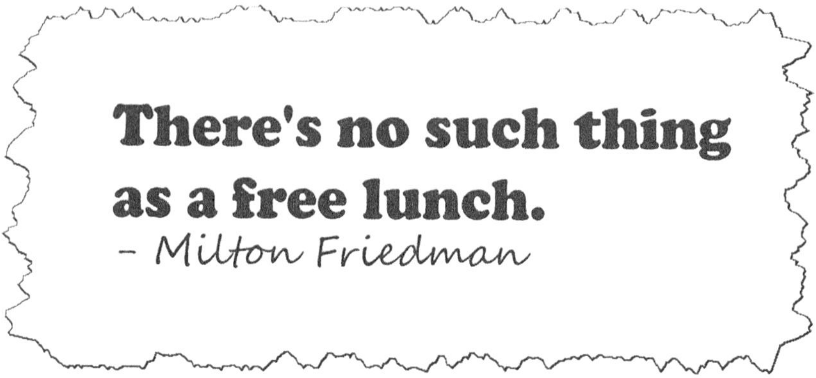

FIGURE 9 - NO FREE LUNCH

"Paying for Lunch" - What is required

The enterprises that are going to thrive and dominate in this information age are the ones that acknowledge the need for a reasonable pace of delivery for information assets. Additionally, they must begin paying down any technical debt that has been accrued and positioning themselves to be nimble and accurately informed going forward.

A Path Forward

Canonical Information Model

It is possible to understand the business's information requirements, create a technologically agnostic architected model of those information requirements, and use it to drive system implementations, system integrations, reporting, and analytics. In addition, this model can be used as a "universal translator" between systems and businesses to allow more streamlined onboarding of new contributing systems and speed up the data usage by interested parties.

One of the most valuable aspects of a conceptual information model is its long-term value as a business reference and technological bridge. Technologies come and go, but a technologically agnostic model of the business information requirements can persist as a valuable reference and be updated as regulatory requirements change or business strategies evolve.

> **Familiar things happen, and mankind does not bother about them. It requires a very unusual mind to undertake the analysis of the obvious.**
>
> - *Alfred North Whitehead,*
> *Science and the Modern World, 1925*

FIGURE 10 - ANALYSIS OF THE FAMILIAR

Semantic clarity for critical terms with a broad scope

The essential activity (defining terms clearly) is not a new or radical idea and within that fact lies part of the challenge. Creating definitions for key business terms is hard work. The effort required makes most executives, project leaders, and developers try to skip the task (e.g., "Everyone knows what Product means.") Consequently, insufficient time gets allocated to what they perceive as of little value. The sad reality is that no other activity will yield a more significant return on investment over time than establishing canonical definitions for all terms and data elements of broad interest to the enterprise.

Canonical Vocabulary

A canonical vocabulary will speed up:

- system implementations/development
- business negotiations
- business process discussions
- analytics
- reporting
- artificial intelligence implementations
- data science activities
- integration work (internal and external systems)

What can justify neglecting an asset that promises this kind of ***return on investment***?

Reduce Development Time and Mistakes

Reducing development project rework and bug fixes and increasing the speed in realizing contracted interfaces (both internally and externally to partner systems) should be enough to cost-justify the investment of time, effort, and resources dedicated to collecting the definitions before building systems and data structures.

Establish accountability for Enterprise Information efforts

However, it is vital to establish deliverables and timelines for the Conceptual Information Modeling activities and hold the information architects accountable for delivering useful insights and artifacts. Over the years, many of the "Enterprise Data Model" efforts failed because they devolved into predominantly intellectual exercises. The groups became havens for theoretical purists that cared more about philosophical exactitude than actionable work products.

Get ahead of need in Enterprise Information Modeling

The Conceptual Information Architects need to assess the direction of the business, current and future software, and technological implementations and anticipate the information domains that need to be analyzed and modeled in advance of the actual development and implementation projects. The goal is to have predicted the data needs of projects before they start and to be able to deliver solid semantic descriptions and a conceptual model of the information that is needed to be handled by these development teams.

Establish accountability for the Business in supporting Enterprise Information

While it is critically important to hold the Enterprise Information modeling efforts accountable, motivating the business to be active and enthusiastic participants in evolving the Conceptual Information Model is equally vital. The essentiality of active involvement of the business is because the capture of the Conceptual Information Model is very much a team effort. And the business experts are the source of the "raw materials" (business knowledge) that the architects should leverage to build the "mirror" of the business information requirements represented by the Conceptual Information Model.

Build Bridges

If one thing has become glaringly apparent in dealings with information projects globally, when it comes to data and information quality, "simple is not easy." Pushing to do the right thing without reading the room and couching the message in a way that is acceptable to the majority will, in most cases, result in opposition that would make Machiavelli proud. This resistance is because the strategic investment required to gain the long-term value that quality data represents is always in conflict with the tactical or short-term gratification that functioning software implementations appear to display.

To the extent possible, it is vital to maintain good relationships with the I/T development teams and consistently communicate the reasons for investing in reliable information. The long-term and the short-term benefits to the developers and analysts must be effectively shared and reinforced regularly. Enterprises can only achieve long-term improvements in information quality when "hearts and minds" have been swayed in that direction. Without that epiphany, the constant drive to take short-cuts and deliver flashing lights faster will inevitably overwhelm any scruples, and the data universe will succumb to entropy.

The following modern fable will demonstrate some of these interactions and how they might play out and illustrate some tactics and approaches to deal with them.

THE CONSULTING DATA OBSESSIVE [PT 1]

My name is John Thawson, but my friends call me "JT." I've worked in I/T for about 10 years now, and I'm still excited to go to work each day, so I think I made the right career choice. We never had a lot of extra money when I was growing up, so I knew that whatever I decided to study in college would have to support me once I graduated. I started studying accounting in business school, but 30 minutes over an accounting text was like an hour sitting on a toaster oven. Fortunately, our business school required an introductory course in computer programming. And when I discovered that time seemed to fly by when I was working on my programming projects, I figured that would be a better way to spend my working days. So, after a switch in majors, I began my path on a life in I/T.

I recently moved back to Fort Worth, Texas, to care for my mother. My father passed away several years ago, and a year ago, my mother's mental state began to decline rapidly, and she required full-time care.

In what had seemed like a blessing at the time, Mycroft industries aggressively recruited me to come work on their new data initiative. The promotion and salary increase would allow me to provide my mother the care she needed, and their location in the same city where she lived made my decision easy.

So, I packed up my basset hound Winston, loaded my worldly possessions into a U-Haul, and headed for Fort Worth.

The facilities at Mycroft were beautiful, the technology cutting-edge, and the people were very welcoming. I was settling in and looking forward to accomplishing great things.

A week ago, I received some bad news. My new boss (the one that had so aggressively recruited me and for whom I was so excited to work) received an offer to be the Chief Data Officer for another firm and accepted. He seemed apologetic when he told me, and while we both knew that the opportunity was too good for him to pass up, I couldn't help feeling a bit "set up" and betrayed. To make matters worse, when I asked who would be taking his role, he hesitated, and I got a bad feeling.

My boss had approved my shadowing an experienced information engineer, Mr. Hector Leonard Sholks, "Hec," on one of his projects for a week as a training exercise. In light of the new circumstances, I asked my boss if I should cancel the week with Hec, but he said he had gotten it cleared with my new manager, and I should be good to go.

It was with all of this on my mind that I headed out that sunny, if abnormally brisk late fall morning down Baker Street to meet Hec. I was a bit anxious because I had a lot of respect for "Hec." I had been following him on social media and his blog for a while. He first caught my attention with his assertion that data and information were completely different things and, as such, should be architected and managed independently of each other. It took me a while to separate the idea that the requirement existed separately from the design. Still, when it clicked, I began to dig deeper into Hec's philosophies and approach to I/T architecture and found some intriguing ideas. He even said that the Chief Data Officer role should not be in I/T but instead report to the organization's business side. Of course, these statements were considered heresy by some and incited a bit of controversy. Nevertheless, I was still trying to wrap my head around the ideas and the arguments, both pro and con.

I was already becoming aware of some of the new professional challenges I'd face in my new role and desperately needed some inspiration and guidance. So when, during our email exchanges, Hec offered me the opportunity to ride along on one of his engagements, I jumped at the chance. Surprisingly, when I explained what I would be doing to my boss, he agreed to let me spend the initial week with Hec as a work assignment and training opportunity. He knew of Hec and believed that the experience would be beneficial. He had brought me into the company to be his Senior Data Architect for a new data initiative that was kicking off. I think he wanted me as fully informed as possible.

I was challenged by several aspects of our data, best summarized by the number of Vs of data you choose to acknowledge: Volume, Variety, Velocity, Veracity, Variability, etc. The last time I checked, I think someone had come up with 10 Vs over which data professionals could obsess. Still, frankly, the only "V" I was concerned about right now was the Viability of my career as a thought-leader around data topics.

I had enjoyed a great deal of success in a technical career path. I had advanced steadily and rapidly from entry-level developer to senior developer, DBA, then data architect, and now the next logical step was assuming some leadership in data architecture. I was excited to add a new dimension of thought leadership, methods, and skills and take on new challenges. Still, I had been a bit taken aback when I began to understand the scope of the expectations and flawed assumptions that executive leadership in our company had about data.

Mycroft Industries

Mycroft Industries is a large international technology supplier with three main divisions: Personal Devices, Cloud Services, and Consulting Services spanning the globe as divided up into three major geographical regions: Americas, Europe/Middle East/Africa [EMEA], and AsiaPacific. Over 40 years of growth by acquisition without integration has resulted in a phenomenally diverse collection of data repositories, including six full-blown instances of a robust accounting package ("Copper Beeches" Enterprise Resource Planning [ERP] software) operating independently. Layer on all the functionally siloed application development performed over that period, and you come up with a data swamp that reeks of bubbling sulfur and dead things.

Attempts to pull insights from this cauldron of complexity are tedious, uncertain, and error-prone. Additionally, multiple previous attempts to integrate our internal systems and data repositories and build electronic bridges to our external service providers have failed. Nevertheless, the organization appears to have finally realized that something different is required. However, there remains a significant amount of debate over what is needed.

The I/T group is a challenge because from entry-level programmers to senior executives, there is the belief that there is a software solution to our data quality issues. They assert that we just have not bought the right software or put the right technology in place.

Unencumbered by any real awareness of the actual horrific state of our data universe, recently, executive leadership on the business side became excited about "data lakes." It seems a slick salesperson had convinced them that leveraging the 40 odd years of historical business data and the vast quantities of data from external sources would be a snap if they'd bring his team onboard. So they had begun speaking in excited tones about our 'data lake', and again, unchallenged by reality, they were thrilled to start dredging for gold there.

Mycroft Industries Data Vision

In my initial discussion with my new boss, the newly appointed Director of Data Services, Mary Jane Carruthers or "MJ" to her friends (Ms. Carruthers to me), she blithely rattled off the list of capabilities desired: "Predictive Analytics, Machine Learning, Artificial Intelligence, Internet of Things connectivity, Full-Sale-Cycle Real-Time Dashboard, Global Real-Time Supply Chain monitoring, Blockchain-enabled contracts, streamlined regulatory compliance (we had just lost a privacy lawsuit) and a flexibly 'future-proofed architecture."

So, rather than a formal vision statement, we had a laundry list of pet projects and a wish-list of technologies collected from various senior executives to drive our efforts. To demonstrate how serious they were about the initiative, they decided to set up a "Tiger Team" to address it.

Ms. Carruthers asked me to lead the cross-functional NextGen Data Tiger Team tasked with reshaping Mycroft Industries into a data-driven enterprise and implementing the infrastructure to enable it. The system we were to implement was named the "Mycroft Online Reporting and Information Asset Retrieval Technological Interface [MORIARTI]." The intent was to automate the policies, procedures, and assets to support all the latest and greatest data-related technologies and capabilities while positioning Mycroft Industries to rapidly onboard future data-dependent innovations effectively and inexpensively.

To avoid surprise information requirements to the developers and ensure that the business actively engaged with our team, I requested representatives from I/T and the business to be team members in the Tiger Team to facilitate communication and keep everyone up to date.

I/T contributed one senior platform architect (John Clay) that had a deep understanding of the current technology stack's features, requirements, and constraints and a solid understanding of the desired future-state technologies under consideration. Additionally, the Scrum Masters for the four major I/T projects underway were designated to facilitate cross-team communication and awareness of data issues.

The business chose to send a single somewhat junior resource (Ahmso Greene), with the stated intent that the person would act as a "conduit" between our team and the business and develop an understanding of the business in the process of the communication. Their justification was that all their "senior" (experienced) businesspeople were too busy to get involved in what they considered an I/T project, which was not their responsibility or priority. So, Ahmso was the resource that they could spare for our project.

This approach proved to be incredibly inefficient, as Ahmso effectively never had any of the answers required and had to take everything down as an action item and follow up. Furthermore, the follow-up process was highly inefficient, and getting credible feedback typically took several back-and-forth iterations.

Additionally, the definitions of the information elements we were collecting would effectively drive the subsequent data validation, edits, and usage of the data elements in question, therefore defining how the business would operate. Since Ahmso was not authorized to make business policy decisions, the process of refining the information descriptions became mired quickly.

It became clear that we would need to request a more senior business representative for the business as a whole and a business SME from each significant project to mirror and partner with the Scrum Masters to keep business and I/T in sync.

In addition to the challenges of getting the business involved, I was frustrated by an ongoing struggle with John Clay about constructing our draft data model. The conflict essentially centered around John wanting to structure the data to optimize the performance of the current technology stack. Still, I'd learned the hard way that optimizing for one particular technology or one specific business use case would almost certainly "de-optimize" the structure for future technologies and other transactions. Furthermore, this de-optimization would add more technical debt to an already oppressive burden. I was dearly hoping to start making things better rather than continuing our downward slide into chaos. However, our executive leadership team demanded that John and the developers deliver functioning systems in compressed timeframes. The executives were disinterested in anything but their immediate delivery milestones, none of which included information or data quality assessments/signoffs.

As we began the kickoff and visioning discussions, as a new leader in this little circus, I was keenly interested in figuring out what was essential to each player to effectively include their wishes as a part of whatever solution we recommended. But observing the team's interactions, I noticed a discouraging trait in almost all of them. Every participant that was putting forward alternatives seemed entrenched and not listening to anyone else's ideas. They had made up their minds about what they wanted and the best way of getting that, and all they were listening for when the other parties were speaking were weak points to attack to undermine the other party's position.

I was painfully aware that if we were to be successful, I would have to acquire a whole new set of not specifically technological skills, and I found that prospect a bit daunting, to be honest.

Adding new skills was nothing compared to the stress of an unknown quantity for a boss and needing this job to work out so I could afford to take care of my mother. I had found an excellent assisted-living facility right on the way from the office to my house.

The Baker of Baker Street

Breakfast

So, it was with all this keeping me up nights and nagging my waking hours that I arrived at "The Baker of Baker Street" that morning. The company had engaged Hec to evaluate and provide recommendations regarding their desire to become a data-driven enterprise. We had agreed to meet at their flagship café storefront to get a look around, have breakfast, and discuss the opportunity at hand before going in and meeting with the executive leaders and business subject matter experts.

As I walked through the front door to the café and scanned the counter area looking for Hec, the combined aromas of coffee and warm pastries tantalized my senses, and I felt my stomach rumble a bit as I'd held off on breakfast in anticipation of this meeting. The chalk menu board was a colorfully artistic masterpiece boasting such entries as: "Seven Percent Solution Java," "The Scones of Baskerville" in a variety of flavors, and a red-velvet cupcake named "A Study in Scarlet." A beautiful assortment of every pastry imaginable filled the glass display cases. The baristas were moving like automatons, steaming milk, calling orders, and banging the espresso machine portafilters to empty the used grounds for recycling, refilling them, and starting the process all over again.

I heard someone call my name to the right of the waiting area, and I turned to see Hec holding up his hand from a two-top table next to the window. He smiled and gestured for me to join him, and I headed that way, carefully making my way around the assembled patrons waiting for their coffee orders.

"Hec?" I verified as I reached the table, and his smile and nod reassured me that I was not accosting some stranger in a public place. "This place is a bit of a madhouse, isn't it!?" I observed as I set my bag down and pulled back my chair. "Yup! I take that as a good sign for the likelihood of their being able to pay my invoice!" he replied with a chuckle.

Hec looked much like his online profile photo, mid-60s, tightly trimmed silver hair with a somewhat incongruous goatee and deep tan. He wore blue jeans, a black polo shirt, forest-green houndstooth sport coat, black cowboy boots, and a black newsboy cap. His easy drawl was unmistakably Texan. Hec had worked out of the Austin, Texas area for the last 30 years, and his tanned face indicated that he managed to get outside frequently. His easy manner and ready chuckle quickly put me at ease.

"I hope you are hungry," he said, gesturing toward the table where an impressive assortment of pastries and beverages awaited. "When I told them that we would be meeting here to prepare for our morning meeting with them, they insisted on buying us breakfast. It pays to choose one's clients carefully; it appears.", he said with a smile. I agreed wholeheartedly, and we settled in to enjoy the feast.

"Do you mind if we talk business while we eat?" Hec queried. "Not at all," I mumbled around a mouthful of "Blue Carbuncle" blueberry muffin. Hec smiled and pulled out a manila folder covered in notes, highlighter, and sticky notes and laid it in the seat of an unused chair that he pulled over from a nearby four-top table.

"' The Baker of Baker Street, LLC' was established in 2015 as a labor of love by Ms. Ranee Idler. After a successful career as an efficiency consultant, Ms. Idler inherited a small fortune from her grandmother upon her passing. One of the fondest memories of Ms. Idler's youth was breakfast at her grandmother's kitchen, and she decided to share the pastries that had been a big part of those breakfasts with the harried citizens of Fort Worth as they made their way to work."

Hec continued, "Ms. Idler's experience with optimizing processes served her well, and she soon had outgrown her initial operation (based in this same storefront) and was opening locations across the city. As her business grew, so did her need for effective automation and I/T support for her operations and financial needs. Up to this point, they have successfully operated using a desktop accounting software package and standard office software tools, but as the temptation to expand into more locations has grown, so has the acknowledgment that more robust data processing and information resources are required."

"In the course of working with her clients over the years, Ms. Idler witnessed the problems caused by organically evolved siloed data solutions. She is committed to avoiding making the same mistakes at Baker and has asked me to come in and do an assessment and lay out a path forward to turn The Baker of Baker Street into a state-of-the-art information-driven enterprise. It is with that in mind that she has asked us here this morning for some initial discussions."

"We are in a somewhat unusual situation here, as the owner and CEO of the organization is directly engaging us, based on her desire to do the 'right thing' regarding information in the enterprise. I honestly cannot ever remember having a similar opportunity presented to me. Typically, the push for information quality starts at a lower level in the executive 'food chain' after some form of analytics or report results don't make sense, and someone raises an alert. Then the infighting and political maneuvering start over every single policy, procedure or standard proposed in an attempt to clean it up."

I nodded as Hec described this scenario because it was almost a word-for-word description of the situation at Mycroft Industries. It seemed like all the executives smiled and nodded enthusiastically in the joint assessment meetings that created the NextGen Data team and then immediately went out and began scheming about how to undermine us and hinder our effectiveness.

Our Agile development teams screamed bloody murder about being asked to gather information requirements before beginning their sprints. They wailed about how it amounted to "Big Design Up Front" and sneered about how we should try to evolve out of the eighties.

Our Enterprise Resource Planning [ERP] group waved their hands imperiously at us when we requested definitions for their data elements and said, "Oh, Copper Beeches provides definitions for all their data elements! So, we're good!" Unfortunately, upon further investigation, we discovered the definitions in many cases to be merely a restatement of the data element name. In other instances, the descriptions were so ambiguously worded as to allow almost anything to be input into the field. To complicate the problem further, most of the people we were interacting with were also the people who had done the initial implementations. Remember, there were six separate implementations done over the years, so many of the original team members had moved on. The remaining participants were well aware of their "critical resource" status and leveraged it to the fullest. Questions about the quality or completeness of the definitions resulted in defensive reactions to perceived assaults on their professionalism.

When executive leadership requested the ERP Group to designate someone to participate in the "NextGen Data" group, the initial reaction consisted of dismissive huffs and cries of "We're too busy!". Finally, however, even the executive leadership most sympathetic to their perspective admitted that ERP data was essential to include in our scope and insisted they provide at least one representative.

Fortunately, the person (Duncan Ross) designated to be a member of the NextGen Data team seemed interested in working out a solution. He had witnessed the problems of connecting the multiple instances of Copper Beeches and establishing external connections to other systems and wanted to find a better approach.

From our initial discussions with Duncan, it became clear that he sincerely believed that all the Copper Beeches data had definitions and that they were adequate. Therefore, I hoped that once Duncan saw the questions that remained about the data contents of Copper Beeches, he would see the need to improve the definitions.

I was jerked from my reverie back into the present as Hec began outlining our schedule for the day. "We have an initial kickoff meeting with Ms. Idler and her top executives at nine AM, followed by a break-out meeting at ten-thirty to discuss some issues that they have had with their catering services division. We've left the afternoon open after lunch to be scheduled based on what comes out of the morning's discussions. I hear they have a pretty tasty lunch menu here as well!" he said with a wink.

As we left the café to head into the corporate offices, we met a 20-something woman dressed in an outfit that was a curious combination of business casual and Ren Fair. Her blonde hair was neatly styled in a short bob, and she had a bright smile. She had a small Celtic symbol tattooed on the inside of her wrist and a woven leather bracelet and matching necklace. She almost seemed to bounce as she greeted us. "Good morning, Hec! My name is Lucy Smith, and Ms. Idler asked me to meet you this morning and help get you through security and set up in the conference room. She also asked me to serve as a scribe for all your meetings and facilitate getting any resources you need."

As she said this, her toe caught on the edge of a brick border on the pavement, and she almost fell head-first. Then, regaining her footing, she laughed and said, "Wonderful first impression!". We all laughed, and she guided us through the front door of the offices.

"Well Lucy, what do you normally do for Baker when you aren't serving as the diplomatic corps and concierge?", Hec asked.

"Oh, I'm a rookie developer on Ms. Cathy Summers' team," she replied. "We just delivered a mobile order entry solution that I think you'll be discussing later this afternoon. Since we are in a bit of a lull between projects at the moment, Ms. Idler thought it would be a great opportunity for me to become more deeply involved in the 'guts' of the underlying data foundations that we are building."

She continued, "My background is a little strange for a developer. I trained as a technical writer, but I was always fascinated by coding and enjoyed the quick gratification of seeing a program work. So, when it came time to choose how I would spend the bulk of my work-day, I chose the path that I thought would be the most entertaining."

"Hmmm… strong language skills with a logically trained mind," Hec said, "I think Ms. Idler has been reading my blog…" he trailed off. "In any case, Ms. Smith, welcome to the team, and if you have any questions, please feel free to ask!"

"Thanks, Hec! I sure will! I'm looking forward to learning a lot!" Lucy said as she stumbled over the edge of the revolving door as we entered the building.

As we crossed the lobby to the reception desk, I asked Lucy what she could tell us about the facilities and resources of Baker. "We operate ten retail cafés in the greater Fort Worth area, each with a dedicated bakery operation to ensure the freshness of the product delivered. Additionally, we have a separate high-capacity bakery dedicated to supporting our new catering division that handles corporate events and events like weddings, etc. We have had to set up a brand-new supply chain to handle the acquisition of the required ingredients and packaging and presentation materials from various suppliers in the greater metropolitan area. We also have a fleet of delivery vehicles to transport ingredients from a warehouse facility that we have recently acquired to ensure that we can manage our supplies inventory efficiently. We are rather proud of our operation, and we are trying to do things the right way as well as being highly active in several charitable initiatives in the area."

"It sounds like you are headed in the right direction and have a solid vision to guide you!" I replied.

"Ah, but in the summary email that Ms. Idler sent me, it appears that the rapid growth and the onboarding of new systems capabilities are presenting some opportunities for growth that she would like for us to address as areas of focus," Hec replied with a sly wink.

"They have outgrown their current accounting software and are looking to do an ERP implementation to combine their accounting functions, inventory control, and supply chain functions into an integrated solution. However, Ms. Idler is concerned that they have taken shortcuts that may have long-term strategic costs to the quality of their information management capabilities in a rush to demonstrate rapid progress. Specifically, requests for plan documents and glossaries are being met with resistance from I/T because they follow an Agile methodology and don't want to get bogged down in Big

Design Up Front [BDUF]. While she doesn't want to micro-manage, she wants to ensure that the key artifacts necessary to the ongoing effective operation, maintenance, and growth of the enterprise are not being neglected while they pursue a rapid delivery."

"Additionally, there is a specific challenge pertaining to their new catering order process that they'd like for us to investigate and see if we can offer any assistance. It seems that while Baker has invested a lot of time and effort in their infrastructure, the actual processing to delivery of their catering orders is struggling to achieve the level of efficiency that Ms. Idler expects."

"Interesting," I observed, "Considering her background, I'd think that would be right in Ms. Idler's area of core expertise."

"Agreed, but the business has grown to a size where she is having to deal with so many other issues that she needs help working through some of the specific challenges, and that is where we come in," Hec replied.

Ms. Idler

As we reached the front desk and checked in with the receptionist, Lucy told him who we were and with whom we were to meet. After checking his workstation screen, he had us sign in, handed us two badges, and smiled as he pointed down the hall to the right, "You are in the main conference room on the left down this hall. 221b. You can't miss it." We took our badges, thanked him, and headed down the hall.

"Well, they are certainly staying true to their branding with their naming, from product names to meeting rooms," Hec said as we entered the front of a large room with an impressive conference table commanding the center of the room.

"Indeed, we are." Said a melodious female voice from the back of the room.

Startled, we glanced up to see a striking woman in a black tailored business suit rising from a chair in the corner. "Hec, this is Ranee Idler. Ms. Idler this is Hec Sholks." Lucy said. Ms. Idler said, "I'm so pleased to meet you, Hec! I've read much of your work."

Her warm smile and sparkling eyes told us that she had not taken offense at our remarks about the conference room name, but Hec quickly said, "I didn't mean any disrespect Ms. Idler; the whole idea quite entertains me; I'm a big fan of Arthur Conan Doyle."

Her smile widened as she said, "Oh, I'm so glad to hear that Hec. I've read and re-read the whole Sherlock Holmes canon multiple times, and it just made sense when I set out on my dream business adventure to incorporate his universe into mine. It was like working with an old friend." She gestured to four seats at the corner of the conference table, and we seated ourselves.

"Lucy has been with us for almost a year now full-time following two very impressive Summer internships with us. I want to get her focused on a data-driven mindset early before any other influences can take too deep a root in her psyche." Ms. Idler said with a twinkle in her eye.

"I remembered your emphasis on the correlation between the structure of language and the architecture of information, and I thought that her technical writing background would make her an ideal fit," she finished.

As Ms. Idler finished, there was a minor crash from the refreshments table as Lucy bumped into the end water bottle causing all the other water bottles to topple like dominoes. "Sorry! Sorry! I'll straighten this up!" Lucy exclaimed.

"You just probably want to keep her away from sharp things…"

Ms. Idler noted with a smile. "She has a powerful mind, infectious enthusiasm, and the lithe grace of a panda bear on a pogo stick."

"But to date, she has demonstrated a consistent heartfelt desire to do what is right for the long-term success of the organization, and that made her stand out to me from the rest of our recent college hires. They were all intent upon getting ahead, even if short-cuts were involved. Not necessarily evil or criminal things, but things that were just a tad too clever." she continued.

"Lucy has a curious mind and a directness that she may have to learn to control over the long haul but which makes her trustworthy and dependable. I hope that being involved in all of your meetings and functioning as scribe, she will begin to learn how you think and pick up the basics required to be an advocate for data issues among her peers when you are not on the premises." Ms. Idler concluded.

"That sounds like a splendid plan, and I'll make sure she has all of my contact information and knows that she can contact me anytime with any questions she may have," Hec replied.

Ms. Idler continued, "Now, I wanted to greet you this morning, make sure you were comfortable with Lucy as a team member, and make the initial introductions to the senior leadership team with whom you will be working. But, first, I want to make sure that we've established your credentials to them. They are great people and have extremely sharp minds, but from time to time, they can be a bit shark-like with newcomers, and I need for them to know that you are speaking for me on this issue", she said with a wink.

"We have grown as fast as we have because of the smart decisions, hard work, and focused execution that these ladies and gentlemen have brought to bear on our vision. However, the proliferation of data siloes, our struggles to maintain our quality of data, and our attempts to bring all of the various collections into a single cohesive reflection of reality have begun to trouble me a bit. I fear that as we grow, it will only become a bigger and bigger issue as we begin to include massive quantities of external data from social media and our business partners if we don't get out in front of it."

"The meeting that you will be facilitating at 10:30 right after our kickoff introductory meeting represents one of the symptoms of the problem that we have identified. We have an order process pretty clearly defined for our catering business, but we are struggling mightily to make it function effectively."

"We have wrestled with this issue for a few weeks now, and nerves are getting frayed, and we've had a few 'direct' conversations that have been less than productive. So I hope that you can engage with all the parties concerned, diagnose the root cause and get us back on track," Ms. Idler smiled hopefully.

Kick-off Meeting

The door opened, and several people began to come in, so we rose to introduce ourselves to the new arrivals as we moved to arrange ourselves around the conference table. Ms. Idler took the seat at the head of the table with Hec immediately to her right, and I took the chair next to him.

The executive leadership team quickly came in with the usual pleasant greetings and good-natured banter and arranged themselves around the conference table in short order.

Ms. Idler started the meeting and did the introductions, and concluded with, "I'm proud of everything that we've accomplished thus far and all the hard work that all of you have contributed to our success. However, we all know that if we are not progressing and growing, we are stagnating and dying, and my greatest concern right now is that the lifeblood of our business operations, our data, is not where we need it to be."

There was a clang from the back of the room, a high-pitched, whispered "Sorry!" and I didn't even have to look to know who it was…

Ms. Idler continued, "I have asked Hec to come in and give us some thought leadership around positioning ourselves to have a data asset base that is…" and she wrote the following on the whiteboard:

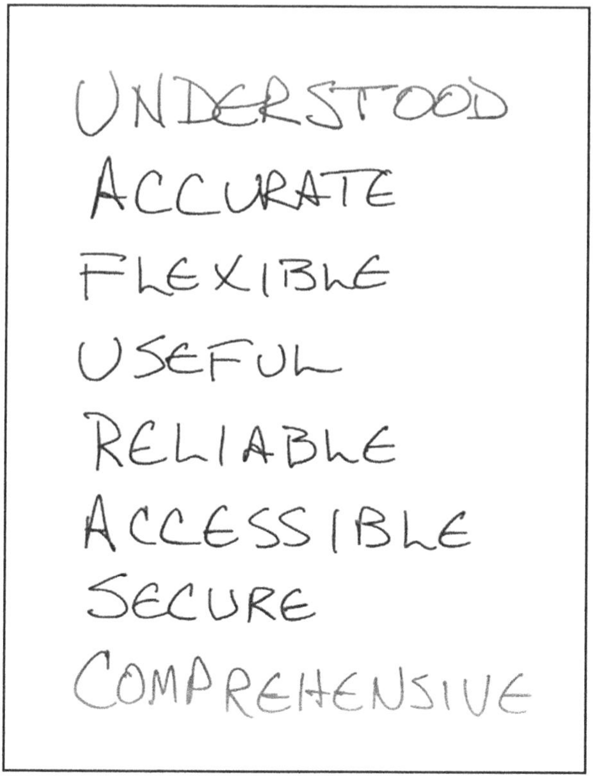

FIGURE 11 - DATA QUALITY VISION WHITEBOARD

"Additionally, we need solid Governance in place to ensure that our data continues to mean what we think it means and that we are handling all our sensitive data per pertinent regulations. We want all our headlines to be happy ones," Ms. Idler said with a smile and was greeted with chuckles.

"Finally, we need to continue to evolve as rapidly as possible, however 'as possible' incorporates the idea of not taking shortcuts that create unreasonable problems for us down the road, so keep that in mind in your discussions," she concluded.

"I have another meeting that I need to get to; does anyone have any questions before I leave you?"

Jacob Parvender, the Director of I/T, asked, "We've got a lot of 'in flight' projects with tight schedules and some that are just starting up… is this going to affect our project timelines?" I notice Hec smile at this.

"I'll refer you back to my earlier comment about 'as fast as possible' for your guideline. We do need our system implementations to continue as quickly as possible. Still, the priority is to create solutions that both provide our immediate tactical needs while strategically positioning us to be able to move faster in the future and with greater effectiveness," Ms. Idler responded. "I assume that there will be some 'give and take' involved in the decision-making process. However, 'tight schedules' need to be constructed to include ALL necessary activities to get us where we need to be. I am guessing that will be one of the key areas of discussion and potential paradigm shifts that come out of all of this. I look forward to hearing what you come up with."

I noticed Hec seemed a bit pleasantly taken aback, and he smiled and offered, "I'm confident we will come up with a plan that moves Baker in the direction desired."

Ms. Idler smiled and nodded as she rose from her chair, "Well, with that, I'll leave you to it… Hec, please lay out for the leadership team the broad strokes of what you plan to do as much as you can in the remaining time, and let's meet again in this room this afternoon at 3:00 pm to discuss strategies, what deliverables you plan to produce, and when." With that, she left.

Hec's Opening Statement

Hec smiled as he rose to face the executive leadership team around the table. "Good morning, folks. In concept, what we need to accomplish here may seem simple after I describe it to you but make no mistake about it; 'simple' does not equal 'easy.'" He paused to let the statement sink in.

"We need to define a clear vision statement for what information-driven means at Baker. Then, we need to identify the key strategies to implement that vision, and once we have all agreed and taken ownership of the vision and the strategies, we need to plan how we are going to pursue those strategies. Simple, right?"

"Here's where simple stops being easy. First, we all need to understand why this vision around information is critical. Second, we all need to agree that the strategies are valid. And third, we all need to commit to staying the course and doing what is right for Baker strategically, even when short-term wins are jeopardized. Getting aligned on this is so critical that if we need to have multiple meetings to reach consensus, then that is what we will do."

Language and Communication

"A great deal of emphasis is going to be placed on effective communication: between humans, between leadership, management and staff, and between systems. Human-to-human and leadership-to-management communication is often assumed to be precise and effective while being based on assumptions and misaligned understandings that, when left unchecked, can result in costly errors when crystallized into data processing systems. We are going to attempt to minimize this gap as much as possible. However, our expectation is not perfection because businesses are still defined and run by human beings. Therefore, we must plan our strategies to be flexible and adaptable to both changing business and legal requirements and error-remediation."

"However, I will offer this aside to any that are concerned about tight schedules that might be affected by any additional requirements work. The process of refining the language and solidifying the definitions of key terms inevitably drives out enough unknowns and assumptions in the form of action items and clarifying questions to the business during the requirements phase that the actual development, testing, and roll-out activities are significantly streamlined."

Language of Leadership vs. Language of Management

"Leadership focuses on the vision, strategies, and direction of the business (i.e., "Where we want to go"), and management focuses on running the process and delivering results (i.e., "How we are going to get there.")."

"It has been noted[1] that because of their specific priorities and perspectives that over time leadership has come to have its own language and management has its own language and at times those two languages do not directly map."

"Compounding the situation, often business units which are focused on optimizing the operations of their specific areas of responsibility evolve their own dialects and siloed systems and data as a practical workaround to satisfy their tactical needs. Additionally, each new software package implemented will have some slightly different perspectives and vocabulary that quickly becomes assimilated by the people using it. Thus, over time, differences in terminology between business units grow if left unchecked, increasing the difficulties in sharing data across business unit boundaries."

Hec took a breath and surveyed the table, "We only need to be sticklers about the Enterprise Business Glossary when we are discussing data elements, processes, or concepts that span the enterprise. Any terminology you choose is acceptable when talking about data elements, processes, or concepts that never extend outside a given business unit."

"However, when discussing data elements, processes, or concepts that are of interest to the whole enterprise, you must employ the Enterprise Business Glossary. That is the only way we will ever be able to integrate our information at the enterprise level."

"An example of this would be in Purchasing. If all you ever deal with are Purchase Orders and everyone calls them 'Orders,' there is no reason to complicate things. However, when addressing the whole company, it is necessary to distinguish 'Purchase Orders' from 'Sales Orders' to avoid confusion, and you must name the enterprise data elements with enough precision to ensure that the distinction is always obvious."

As I looked around the room, although I did see a couple of the executives nodding and smiling, I could tell that Hec had not convinced everyone, and I was a bit uneasy. However, Hec continued.

Data vs. Information

Hec went to the whiteboard and began drawing. As he did, he said, "Many of the conflicts that I've encountered with I/T through the years have stemmed from the synonymous usage of 'data' and 'information' when in fact they are related but very different things. For us to proceed efficiently, we need to get some concepts clearly understood. We use words like data, information, knowledge, and wisdom pretty loosely in our day-to-day discussions. Still, they represent very different stages in the lifecycle of data and information. We must understand the differences because each term has different features, approaches, and requirements. The intellectual giants on whose shoulders I stand thought these things through, and this roughly represents what they came up with." As he finished, he stepped away from the whiteboard to reveal his drawing.

The Wisdom Tree

FIGURE 12 - DATA TO WISDOM TREE

"Data can be thought of as the seeds that grow and mature into information which, when combined, yield Knowledge which, when combined with experience and context yields the fruits of wisdom. Down here at the bottom, we see raw data progressing through its more structured, formatted forms and syntax."

"So, we know we have the number five, and eventually we know that five represents five US Dollars. After we add more context by combining metadata and possibly other data fields, we have the information that 'five dollars' represents the price of a single liter of unleaded gasoline."

"By combining and analyzing other pieces of information, we can develop the knowledge that 'five dollars' is a relatively high price for a liter of gasoline."

"By applying experience and context to our newly acquired knowledge, we can hopefully make the wise decision to pay the price and buy the gasoline if this is the only gas available for the next 200 miles."

"It's helpful to lay things out this way because when I say that our focus is going to be primarily around helping Baker architect the contents of the 'Information' bracket, you can see what we are not going to be doing. I am not here to design your systems, and I'm not here to tell you how to run your business. However, I am confident that Baker has many extremely qualified resources in I/T that can optimize the technology du jour's designs that drive everything in the "Data" bracket. But they should only do that after gaining a clear understanding of the information requirements derived from creating the Information Architecture. I am also confident there are business leaders with the 'wisdom' that understand Baker's business, where it is going, and what is needed to be known (the 'knowledge') to get there. My primary mission is to bridge the gap in business knowledge between the business and the I/T experts by building the Information Model as a reference. However, I/T should implement nothing in the data space without being guided by a requirement in the Information space."

Baker of Baker Street Information Vision

"To stay with the idea of data being seeds that grow into information, I'd summarize the information vision provided by Ms. Idler as '**Cultivate information**.'"

"To cultivate information, we know we need to prioritize understandability, accuracy, flexibility, usefulness, reliability, accessibility, security, and comprehensiveness of the data while governing it to ensure ongoing quality."

"I'd like to make sure that we have a shared understanding of each of the target characteristics of our future state information architecture by writing down descriptions for each of the characteristics that have we have listed."

"Why don't we just look up the definitions online and be done with it?" asked a question from the far end of the table.

Hec smiled, "Thank you for bringing that up. We can do that. Certainly, we can use those descriptions as "seeds" for discussion. However, much like the definitions for our data elements, we want to ensure that the descriptions precisely capture what you, as representatives of Baker, want the word to mean. There is also the sense of ownership and buy-in that comes from agreeing on what each term means."

"So... 'Understandability'... What does that mean?" and we spent the remainder of the meeting collecting definitions for the key terms in the vision statement.

By the time we wrapped up the meeting, we had come up with the following working definitions for our target information architecture qualities:

Understandability - Each data element should be thoroughly and uniquely defined to ensure proper usage and interpretation.

Accuracy - Each data element should have processes to ensure that the values contained therein are correct and current.

Flexibility - Data structures should be built in such a way as to facilitate reuse across existing systems as well as being able to adapt to support future requirements rapidly.

Usefulness - Data collected and maintained should be suitable for and have value to a business usage by the enterprise.

Reliability - Data stores should be structured to ensure they remain available.

Accessibility - Data should be maintained in such a way that all interested parties can get to it.

Security - Data should be protected to ensure that only legitimate users can access it.

Comprehensiveness - Efforts should be made to ensure that all of the required data needed by the business is available.

FIGURE 13 - INFORMATION QUALITIES

Throughout the meeting, I observed some of the previously disengaged executives begin to get involved and seem more engaged as we went along; however, a couple of them still spent most of the meeting glancing at their phones. The most distressing offender, the manager of the I/T developers [Cathy Summer], had been invited along by the Director of I/T purely for informational purposes. She went out of her way to argue that technology would solve all the concerns we had mentioned if she could get more team members and funding. When it became apparent that she wasn't going to derail the discussion, she withdrew for the most part and sat in sullen silence. She did interject at one point that we didn't have time to write down definitions because we had more important things to do than create "useless" documentation. She asserted that it was silly anyway because everyone knew what the core business terms meant. I watched Hec smile quizzically and continue the discussion to the end.

As we adjourned the meeting, Hec closed with, "The only way that a rational professional is going to buy into an idea completely is by seeing it in action and by seeing it deliver results. So I look forward to demonstrating the principles we've discussed and showing real-world results. I hope that all of you will keep open minds and work with us to position Baker for future excellence."

Hec continued, "I believe some of you are in the next meeting in this room where we will be working through an issue that seems to have arisen with the new catering order process. I hope that we can demonstrate some of our key concepts in that meeting. So again, thank you for your time and contributions. I'll see those of you in that next meeting in a few minutes."

After everyone had left and the door had closed, I commented, "I think that Cathy Summer is going to be a challenge."

Hec smiled, "If you watched who Cathy was reacting to and noticed the timing of her contributions, it becomes fairly obvious that Cathy is all about Cathy, has some level of political awareness, and is cautious. She didn't voice her objections while Ms. Idler was in the room, and when she was unable to get the group shifted to her side, she withdrew, for the most part, biding her time and make no mistake about it; she isn't done fighting us. Therefore, we must show her what is in it for her by demonstrating how our approach will allow her to produce more effectively in a visible manner. Otherwise, we will have to resort to using Ms. Idler as a battering ram to clear her out of the way. That is an option of last resort because it can only be used a limited number of times (think "once"). Cathy has demonstrated some value to the organization, or she wouldn't have made it into that room this morning, so we'd rather convert her than eliminate her."

Hec continued, "Most people view themselves as having good intentions and think that they are just trying to get by. Therefore, they feel justified in their actions. It would be hard to imagine anyone seeing themselves as the Bond villain they eventually become in our minds. It is very unusual to run into someone who is being difficult just for the sport of it, although it does happen. Ninety-nine percent of the time, the challenges you have to deal with spring from a spectrum of motives ranging from ignorance at the most innocent extreme through impatience, laziness, stubbornness/arrogance, or greed at the most cynical extreme. You must identify which of your challenging resources are mostly resisting out of ignorance and focus your efforts there first."

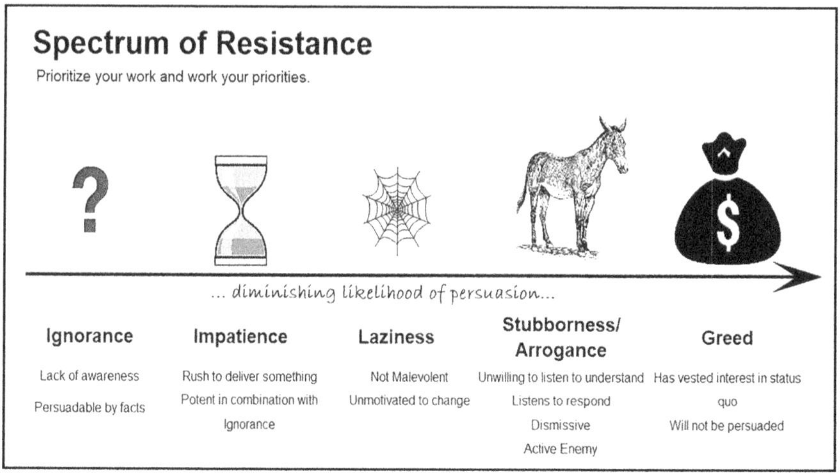

FIGURE 14 - THE SPECTRUM OF RESISTANCE

"The hope would be that Cathy just doesn't 'get it' yet, and after the benefits have been explained and demonstrated, she would come around. However, if her actions indicate her motives lie on that right end of the spectrum, we still will have to deal with it somehow."

"That's all well and good for a situation like this one where you are empowered." I replied, "But how do I deal with this situation operating at a lower level on the organization chart?" I said, thinking back to my debates with John Clay at Mycroft.

"Oh, it can be quite tough and, in many cases, impossible to sway some people from their deeply held convictions, potentially ignorant or lazy thinking, or greed for advancement," Hec replied. "The only thing you can do is be completely prepared for every meeting with as many facts as you can gather, speak to those facts, and consistently demonstrate that you are putting the best interests of the organization first in the positions you take."

"It seems crazy that you can increase your credibility by ceding a point that an opponent has effectively argued. However, as it becomes clear that you are listening to understand and are willing to change your mind based on facts, your credibility with others in the organization will go up. There is also the possibility that your working relationship with your opponent can improve. There is nothing more counter-productive to progress than digging in and refusing to engage. But there are no guarantees. I've been in situations where the party on the other side was so arrogant that they just thought that their arguments were all just too powerful to rebut. Those situations rarely end well. There has to be a give-and-take for there to be any progress."

Hec glanced at the clock and said, "Cathy is going to be in this next meeting, so let's hope that it goes well and that she begins to understand what we are trying to do."

About that time, the door opened, and the participants in the 10:30 meeting arrived.

Hec observed, "We are going to have to delay starting on Strategy briefly while we jump right into some 'doing.' Here's hoping we get some buy-in and traction from this exercise."

Baker Street Day 1 - 10:30 Order Process Meeting

After everyone had seated themselves and pleasantries had been exchanged, Hec stood and said, "Good morning! I think all of you were just here for the kickoff meeting for our initiative to move Baker toward being an information-driven organization, so hopefully, the questions we ask and the perspective that we take won't be too much of a surprise to you."

"It is my understanding from a brief overview that you are experiencing challenges with processing orders for your new catering business. I don't know any details beyond that, so could one of you that is more intimately acquainted with the situation provide an introductory overview?"

After momentarily exchanging glances, the Baker representatives silently agreed that Peter Jones, the Chief Financial Officer for the company, would summarize the situation.

His voice was clear, and his description got right to the point. "Ninety days ago, we rolled out a line of business to provide catering services to customers in the greater metropolitan area. We located our production bakery as centrally as possible, and we have a small fleet of delivery vehicles to rapidly move our finished goods from bakery to consumer. Our supply chain for the ingredients is operating effectively, and our actual production line is performing as expected. However, we are having a real problem in getting our orders through the order process and into the production queue promptly."

Mr. Jones continued, "It is particularly frustrating because we spent a considerable amount of money standing up our 'Wide Area Technical Sales Operations Network.' The idea was to allow our salespeople to enter their orders from their mobile devices and get things started as soon as possible. Ms. Summer and her team were able to get all of the coding done in a short time, and we were able to start entering orders right on schedule."

"With our production and delivery capabilities, we should be able to turn an order around in 24 hours. However, we've had to push back to a five-business day lead because there is so much delay in the current order processing system that we cannot get the orders into the production queue sooner than that."

"The software seems to be working properly. The salespeople can enter the orders and submit them to the system, but then there seems to be a delay and a lot of validation and re-work before the orders go into the production queue."

"Huh..." Hec said. "Can you share what a typical order looks like?" he said as he pointed to the projection screen.

"Sure!" chimed in Cathy Summer as she reached for the projector and switched it on. She then worked on her laptop until an image flashed on the screen at the front of the room.

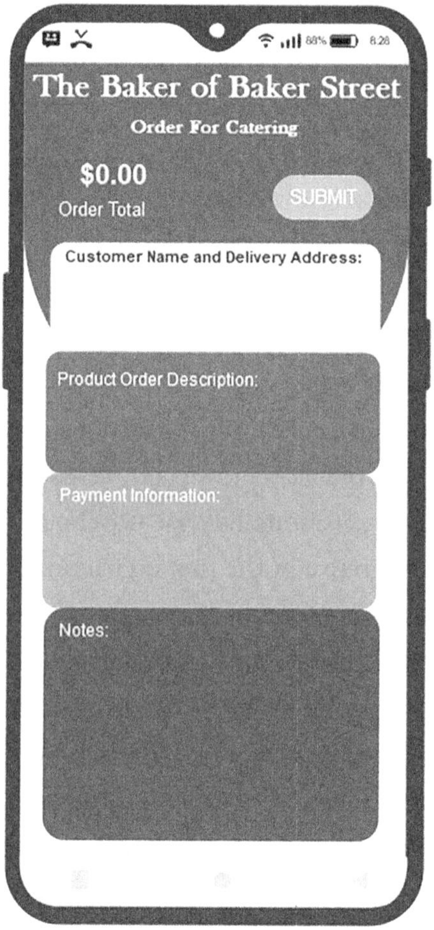

FIGURE 15 - BAKER INITIAL CATERING ORDER SCREEN

As I looked at the screen, some obvious concerns from a data perspective were apparent at a quick look, and I glanced over at Hec, who impassively surveyed the screen layout.

Hec started, "Sooo, perhaps someone could provide some background and context to what we are looking at here. What drove the need for this application, who championed it, and what were the constraints?"

A dapper gentleman in a tailored suit with matching tie and pocket square cleared his throat. "Perhaps I can help with that some. I am Ronald Adair, and I am the Executive Vice-President of Marketing and Sales," he said with a warm smile.

As we smiled and acknowledged his introduction, he continued. "The Baker of Baker Street has experienced a pleasantly surprising rate of growth for our retail outlets, primarily due to the high quality of our product and some very astute location selection."

"We identified an opportunity in the catering sector and embarked upon setting up an additional line of business to pursue that market. Near the end of last year, we completed the acquisition and configuration of our corporate bakery, warehouse and distribution center. We hoped to go live in the first quarter of this year."

"However, as we were working through the process, we realized that the most effective way to have our catering sales representatives enter the orders would be to enable them to use their mobile devices. With time pressing us to be operational, we approached Cathy Summers and her team and asked them if they could have a mobile application running in six weeks, which she agreed to do."

"Cathy and her team worked a miracle and got us a functioning application working in five weeks, and we had a week to roll it out to our fairly small sales team."

"Except it doesn't provide what our automated system needs to deliver the required product, and we have to spend hours trying to get the customer on the phone and work out the details of their order," offered a voice from the far end of the table.

As we turned to face the lean, athletically built gentleman dressed in a crisp business casual outfit of chinos and golf-shirt, he introduced himself, "I'm Alec Macdonald, and I'm Executive Vice-President of Production and Delivery. The problem is, we receive these 'orders' partially filled out or incorrectly filled out. Even worse, when they are close to correct, there is still a ton of work to do to translate them into inputs to our automated Bakery Execution Logistics Line [BELL] that produces the baked goods for our catering deliveries."

"You see, BELL can produce any of our standard baked goods using pre-programmed recipes and automated ingredient handling, but it needs to have a known, standardized product specified and the quantity of the product desired as well."

"Well," Cathy quickly interjected, "we were under a tight time constraint, so compromises were necessary. Therefore, Sales and Marketing agreed that we could just simplify the design by using free form text fields for the data so that we could get it tested and moved into production quicker."

"Because what do they care? They don't have to DO anything with it after they've gotten credit for the sale!" snapped Alec.

Hec quickly rose to the whiteboard and offered, "Why don't we do a little exercise here to see if we can come up with a solution?" The three executives grudgingly relented and took seats around the table.

Hec glanced to Lucy and asked, "Lucy would you be so kind as to scribe for us?" to which she replied, "Certainly," and took out her laptop and opened it.

As he wrote the word "Order" on the board, Hec casually wrote "[Sales]" next to the word "Order" and said, "I've found that in a surprising number of instances that conflict springs from a lack of precision and clarity around the language being used to discuss a given situation. Now I don't think that is the only issue here, but I think that it is part of it."

"First, just to be clear, we are discussing 'sales orders' as opposed to 'purchase orders,' correct?" The participants nodded in agreement.

"Keeping in mind that our goal here is to do what is best for the organization as a whole, let's write down a definition of what a sales order is."

Hec turned to Ronald Adair and said, "Mr. Adair, what would your definition of sales order be?" to which Mr. Adair replied, "Well, an order could be a simple as a signature on a napkin…."

"No, it is NOT!" Alec exclaimed as he slapped his palms down on the table and stood. "We can do absolutely NOTHING with that level of detail… so you may have some sort of gentlemen's agreement at that point, but what you do NOT have, sir, is an ORDER!".

Lucy was so startled by the outburst that she jumped a little and knocked her backpack over, spilling the contents. She quickly scooped them up, replaced them in the bag, and resumed her place taking notes.

No one else seemed to be particularly taken aback by this exchange, and when I glanced at Hec, he winked at me and said to the room, "Well… I do believe we have a place to start."

Once everyone had resumed their seats, we spent the rest of the meeting working through a definition of sales order that encompassed the needs of Sales, Delivery, Finance, and Customer Support.

It turned out that once the salesperson pressed the "Submit" button on the application that the sales order then went to Delivery Support. In Delivery Support, the most junior team members would try to match the products specified in the free-text fields to standardized product offerings. When there were discrepancies, these team members would have to make a follow-up telephone call to the customer to determine the desired products. It was unusual to successfully reach the customer on the first attempt, which meant refining the sales order into a usable state could take days, not to mention any issues that might arise about the payment method.

By the end of the meeting, all participants had agreed that while it served as a good "proof-of-concept," the existing order application did not capture the data required to feed the BELL system properly. Therefore, the group agreed that Ronald Adair, Alec MacDonald, and Cathy Summers would meet with Hec and me in a working lunch meeting to document the data requirements that Cathy and her team could use to deliver release 2.0 of the sales order application.

Blank Pages and Green Fields

Day One Summary & Debrief Meeting

At 3:00 pm, we reconvened in 221b for our day's summary and presentation of findings and path forward. Hec had prepared a matrix with Ms. Idler's stated priorities on one axis and our proposed strategies on the other, and Lucy projected it onto the screen at the front of the room.

Hec began, "Ms. Idler, we met with the Executive Leadership Team this morning and had a nice discussion, and then we met with your Marketing, Operations, and I/T folks this afternoon to work through your challenges with your catering order entry system. We made real progress on the Order Entry system, and I believe that a solid path forward has been defined. We discovered some interesting things through that process that we'll be discussing in a moment."

"I'm recommending that you initially pursue five organizational strategies to establish a solid foundation for your information architecture and then employ the appropriate information strategies based on where you are in this process and what your primary goal is. The organizational strategies are Configure, Communicate, Control, Confirm, and Correct."

"I differentiate between organizational strategies and information strategies because the organizational strategies have to do with establishing the framework inside of which you pursue the information strategies. The organizational strategies apply to any type of project, whereas the information strategies are focused on improving enterprise information quality."

"Of the five organizational strategies, the first, 'Configure' will probably become less active as time passes and the enterprise learns what works, and fewer structural changes are needed. First, however, the reporting structure, initial steps, checkpoints, empowerments, and ground rules need to be identified. Then they need to be ratified and communicated to the organization."

"The other four 'C' organizational strategies are ongoing processes that loop and refine themselves as you learn what works and what is needed."

"Concerning the information strategies, I've prepared the following matrix as a tool to verify that what we are doing applies to the stated vision. I've marked the strategies that address a given priority with a green checkmark. I'll go through the strategies one by one, explain the rationale, and if you have any questions, please ask them."

Priorities\ Information Strategies	Definitions	Conceptual Modeling	Governance
Understandability	✔	✔	
Accuracy	✔	✔	✔
Flexibility	✔	✔	
Usefulness	✔	✔	✔
Reliability			✔
Accessibility			✔
Security	✔	✔	✔
Comprehensiveness	✔	✔	

Baker of Baker Street Operational Information Strategies

Definitions

"Every single data element of significance to the enterprise needs to be defined to eliminate any possibility of synonyms or ambiguities. These definitions should be precise, exhaustive, and understandable. They will provide value to the developers building and maintaining the systems, the business analysts defining business processes, and the reporting end-users and data scientists who eventually have to create meaningful reports and draw conclusions from the gathered data."

"The link between solid definitions and the qualities of understandability, accuracy, and usefulness is apparent."

"However, good definitions provide flexibility by providing a clear understanding of exactly what an element means and all the contexts where it applies."

"Good definitions enhance security by clearly identifying what should be contained in a given data element, allowing solid data quality and security edits while populating the data element. Additionally, a clear understanding of the element's contents can inform access control decisions for securing access to sensitive data elements."

"And finally, the comprehensiveness of the information available can only be effectively assessed when an accurate description of the catalog of what is known is available," Hec concluded.

"Any questions about the reason for the Definitions Strategy?" Hec asked.

No one raised a hand, so Hec continued.

Conceptual Modeling

"The Information Architecture is going to be entirely driven by the business via analysis of documents, artifacts, and Subject Matter Expert interviews. It is completely technology agnostic and represents what the business needs to know. That 'need to know' represents the requirement that drives the design and implementation of the data structures in the eventual solutions implemented by I/T."

"Once this blueprint of what is needed to be known is in place, it is possible to both use it to drive and inform future systems designs as well as serve as a roadmap to integrating current systems."

"This single version of the truth blueprint can serve as a universal translator establishing a canonical representation of each information attribute which can map to all of the current data element designs and to which transformations are specified. If desired, this universal translator architecture can be made real over time in a persisted integration hub (database) or virtually instantiated via data services. The decisions about the technical implementation are a completely separate discussion enabled by the technology-agnostic nature of the information architecture. **As a result, the designs evolve independently of the information requirements**."

"As to the relationship between the Conceptual Modeling strategy and the stated vision, the only vision priorities that Conceptual Modeling doesn't directly impact are reliability and accessibility, primarily because of the technology-agnostic nature of the Conceptual Model."

"**Understandability** is enhanced because the documentation of the business relationships connecting the various conceptual entities helps the business consumers to know exactly how to put the information together to answer their questions."

"**Accuracy** is enhanced because the process of working through the descriptions required to do the Conceptual Model and the business language wording of the relationships validates that the model correctly represents the understanding of the business SME."

"**Flexibility** is derived from the Conceptual Model because the architect captures the information requirements correctly. An adequately normalized Conceptual Model has no technological concessions from previous design decisions to complicate things."

"The process of creating the Conceptual Model allows for a sanity check on just how a given piece of information would be used going forward and validated to be worthy of inclusion, maintenance, and governance."

"The Conceptual Model provides a visual layout of the various categories of information and assists with securing the data by providing a ready reference to what information is available to conversations around access control."

"The Conceptual Model can be used to visually review the comprehensiveness of the information catalog by searching for any missing areas of information that might be of significance to the business."

"Is everyone clear on what the Conceptual Model is and why it is important?" Hec asked.

There were a few skeptical expressions, but no one spoke up, so Hec continued.

Governance

"While we were documenting information requirements and assessing identified issues with the current implementation of the order system, we found a few problems. One disturbing discovery we made was that the developers had implemented the Notes field in the application to allow salespeople to store photo images there."

"One of the salespeople had come up with the idea of just taking a photo of the customer's credit card and storing it in the Notes field rather than going to all the trouble of typing the information into the Payment Information field. This little shortcut was a textbook illustration of the dangers of over-loading a poorly defined or loosely governed data field."

Hec commented, "Notes fields are notorious targets for abuse because of the free-form nature of their contents. They attract every bit of data that isn't analyzed and provided a structured, defined, and governed home in the data architecture."

"Fortunately, we discovered this relatively early in the lifecycle of the application and are remedying it, but the implications were enormous. As a result, Ms. Idler has decided to have a thorough review commissioned of all the customer-facing systems to ensure that no such egregious violation of security is happening elsewhere."

Hec summarized, "This would have exposed Baker to both civil and regulatory liability and could have done significant damage to the reputation and brand of the business."

Data Oversight & Governance Group [DOGG]

"To begin managing and securing our data as the asset it is, we will be establishing a Data Oversight & Governance Group [DOGG] to be the clearinghouse for all data-related issues. The process of managing and securing our data includes adding a checkpoint before design and before the first sprint in any Agile project that touches data in any manner. The Doggies,..." Hec smiled, " ...will need to sign off on any project indicating that the data requirements are sufficiently understood and documented to proceed."

"The DOGG should be chaired and run by a data/information

specialist. In addition, it should have representatives from the major business units to represent the information needs of the business and from I/T to facilitate cross-platform communication and ensure that all of the in-flight projects are aware of any identified issues or changes to data structures."

At this point, Jacob Parvender looked past Hec to Ms. Idler and interjected, "As I mentioned earlier, we have several large projects 'in flight' that have pretty tight delivery schedules. Therefore, I don't think we can afford to add additional checkpoints if we are going to keep on schedule."

Ms. Idler smiled and said, "Jacob, I appreciate your diligence regarding delivery and schedule. Are you sure that all of the information requirements for these projects are thoroughly understood and documented?"

The look on Mr. Parvender's face was priceless and indicated that he knew that Ms. Idler had cornered him. If he said "Yes," then the response would be, "Well, then the review of them shouldn't cause too much of a delay." If he said "No," then the response would be, "Then why on earth would we proceed with implementing systems where we are unsure if we are getting the data that we need?"

He opted to deflect and said, "Well, I'm sure there are always additional documents that we could generate. However, we are pursuing an Agile methodology to avoid the unnecessary wasted time associated with generating useless documents associated with Big Design Up Front."

Hec interjected, "Mr. Parvender, are you using off-shore remote developers?"

"Yes, we are optimizing our development spend with off-shore resources." Mr. Parvender replied.

"Are you providing these developers with data dictionaries with full definitions of the data elements that they are implementing?" Hec asked.

"Well, I don't know." Mr. Parvender replied.

"Oh, I know the answer to that one, Mr. Parvender, we aren't providing data dictionaries, per se, but we do provide them with schema layouts of the data structures." Lucy chimed in with a helpful smile. Mr. Parvender struggled to maintain a neutral expression as he smiled at Lucy and said, "Thank you, Lucy!"

Lucy, apparently missing the tension in his face, smiled sweetly and said, "Oh no problem! Happy to help!" and I noticed Sally lean over and whisper something in Lucy's ear, after which she looked a bit taken aback and focused on her laptop screen.

Hec continued, "Mr. Parvender, I have worked from schema layouts in the past. I can tell you that I am confident that we can provide a value-add to your process that will not only reduce your overall bug count but provide a net increase in your development activities. Every time a data element gets used, the developer has a definition of the content in mind; they have to have a definition in mind to figure out how to use that element. That definition can be one that business experts have validated and written down so that every developer understands and uses that element the same way. If not, the definition will be one that each developer derives from context, word-of-mouth, clues, or guesswork. In this latter scenario, until someone takes the time to write down the definition, the process of ferreting out the meaning of that data field will have to be repeated every time it gets used. The problem is, if that definition is not persisted in some manner, for example, written down in a data dictionary, so that the next person to use that data element can refer to it, the definition derived may not match the first definition exactly. Over time, this has a 'whisper game' effect on the contents of the data element, and wide variances can occur resulting in bugs, bad data, and expensive erroneous conclusions."

Hec concluded, "However, I will offer this. Initially, the only check in that DOGG checkpoint will be for clear data definitions for the in-scope data elements. There will not be any other documentation required initially. We want to ensure that the data we are processing is completely understood and that we have thoroughly documented that understanding. We want to make sure that everyone can understand it the same way, from developers to eventual report-writers, data scientists, and executives. I do not think that is an unreasonable request, do you?"

Mr. Parvender shrugged and offered, "I guess not. We'll just have to see how things work out."

Hec smiled, "I am optimistic about the outcome."

I thoroughly enjoyed my week working with and learning from Hec. Lucy turned out to be an absolute joy as a teammate. In addition to being bright, engaged, and curious, she had a wicked sense of humor that kept us in stitches. I had a twinge of regret as the week drew to a close, but I was excited to get back to Mycroft and try my hand at applying the lessons I'd learned.

APPROACHES
[Plan it]

Metamorphosis [Full Buy-in]

Wisdom consists not so much in knowing what to do in the ultimate as in knowing what to do next.
- Herbert Hoover, Readers' Digest, July 1958

FIGURE 16 - WISDOM

It is important to be clear that a complete transformation to an Information-Driven Enterprise as described here is a fundamental shift in priorities across the entire organization. It is an ongoing program from the highest leadership level to the newest individual contributors, not a one-time project.

It is not something an unempowered individual contributor can accomplish, regardless of his or her intellect or other gifts. It cannot be tossed over a wall and forgotten. For the transformation to succeed, preparation, support, communication, great resolve, and commitment to the new approach are required. There will be any number of shortcuts and "emergencies" that will arise. Each will present the opportunity to surrender and make a decision that, if not wholly undermining the goal of the effort, will at least diminish the value of the final result.

We will describe two paths to building the information-driven enterprise. First, we present an entirely strategic transformation initiative for the lucky few that find themselves in the enviable position of being chartered and empowered to shift the enterprise to an information-driven paradigm ("Metamorphosis"). And second, we describe a more tactical insurgent approach ("Incremental Improvement") to support the (more common) poor souls that find themselves in a situation where they have to struggle for every bit of information quality that they can achieve. Finally, we will share some pragmatic tactics that will help show some incremental improvements.

Whichever path you choose, some fundamental tools are needed, and we cover those in "Do it."

Vision Statement

The goal of this book is to assist you in the establishment of an information-driven enterprise capable of effective operational support, reliable and timely analytical activities, assimilation and implementation of new technologies, rapid and effective compliance with evolving regulatory requirements, and the discovery of new insights via support of data science, machine learning, and predictive analytics.

Shifting from a software-driven enterprise to an information-driven one will involve a significant "change management" initiative. Change management is not the only thing involved, but it is the biggest challenge to be faced. The Kallman brothers describe the best path to delivering successful organizational change that I have found in their book on FLOW[1]. Changing the hearts and minds of everyone in the enterprise to let go of historical work patterns and thought processes is a daunting task, but an actual change needs to happen. It is helpful to use the "Five Cs" to frame the necessary steps to effect the change management required to enable an information-driven enterprise: **Configure**, **Communicate**, **Control**, **Confirm**, and **Correct**.

Strategies

Configure

If an enterprise desires to become "data-driven," it is vital that they stop treating data as an after-thought or a by-product. As a result, enterprises are beginning to designate a "Chief Data Officer" [CDO]. Still, the organizations typically position the role in I/T reporting to a "Chief 'Information' Officer" [CIO]. The enterprise measures the CIO's effectiveness on technology-specific metrics (e.g., "system uptime," "data throughput," "network security," etc.). In this situation, concerns about data/information quality will always be considered a hindrance to progress. After an initial "honeymoon" period, the CIO will begin to de-emphasize the CDO's priorities in favor of the rapid implementation of new systems and technologies.

A solution is to:

1. Move the "Chief Data Officer" role out of I/T and onto the business side of the enterprise. Data quality is a priority of the business, and the CDO should focus on the content of the system's data flows and not the technologies.
2. Position the Chief Data Officer at a level in the organization on par with the Chief Information Officer. The Chief Data Officer should be empowered to stop any project or systems implementation in its tracks if the information requirements are not fully understood and documented.

After restructuring the enterprise to be information-driven, it is possible to optimize the process that fulfills new information requirements. There is a basic need to shift from being driven by technology marketing and slick salespeople to evaluating each new initiative based on the incremental insights and capabilities that they will provide. There will undoubtedly be new capabilities provided by evolving technology, but not every new technology will provide a level of incremental benefit to justify the disruption to the organization and, in particular, the additional risk to the cohesiveness and stability of the information ecosystem. I/T must integrate each newly added system with the information ecosystem (at least the parts that handle information of an enterprise scope in value) to maintain the completeness of the end-to-end information collection.

Communicate

Senior leadership must emphatically inform the entire enterprise that "information" (versus business processes, applications, and massive data collection) is the new priority. Information is the priority when acquiring new systems and data sources, delivering new systems and capabilities, scheduling deliveries, and assessing results in the future.

It is not sufficient to communicate this message once in a big rah-rah kickoff meeting. Everyone will frantically nod to show just what great team players they are and then promptly return to business-as-usual as soon as all the cake is gone. This process must be a continuous messaging effort reinforcing the critical value of data quality and information availability. (See: "Above all, sell, sell, sell...")

Along with regularly communicating the message about the importance of information to the enterprise, daily actions and decisions must reinforce the value of the effort and the leadership's commitment to achieving the necessary change. Employees are savvy and will note that executives prioritize short-term gratification over long-term success and adjust their behaviors accordingly. Therefore, if it becomes evident that the newly communicated priority around information is merely posturing, any hope of shifting the organization to an information-driven enterprise is lost.

Control

Entropy is a constant of the universe, and nowhere is that more a certainty than in the data universe of an organization. The successful implementation of integrated information architecture in any organization triggers an auto-immune response, and attempts will immediately begin to circumvent or corrupt it. Every proposed shortcut will be worded in the most persuasive language possible, invoking the mission-criticality of the project in question. If an organization is not fully committed to maintaining strategic focus and no group is empowered to defend the integrated vision, the forces of entropy will prevail. Unchecked, project teams will erode all progress in providing strategic value from the enterprise data until maximum entropy exists.

A governance organization is essential. The business should chair the governance organization, with attendance and participation by I/T. The governance organization should ensure that projects to stand up new systems perform due diligence on all data elements in scope and that they are completely understood and aligned with the information needs of the business, and that data is secured and cataloged.

Initially, this governance organization should frequently meet to get processes and criteria established. After the initial startup phase, the governance organization should meet periodically to provide an opportunity for cross-team communication and interaction, probably every week at a minimum.

Confirm

Any project manipulating existing data or bringing new data into the scope of the enterprise should have a checkpoint/review milestone before the first sprint (or first design meeting). The review should ensure that the information requirements supported by the project are entirely understood, documented, and aligned with the business's needs.

Correct

The business needs to have specific Service Level Agreements (SLAs) defined for how quickly they must respond with a resolution/answer to any questions or discrepancies encountered in the checkpoint review. This accountability is only fair. If we require I/T projects to respect the checkpoint process, then the business must operate with a sense of urgency to get the I/T teams past the checkpoint responsibly as soon as possible.

Again, information is a business priority. The business needs to take responsibility for information quality and be empowered to stop a project in its tracks if the information requirements appear rushed, inaccurate, or incomplete.

The strategies outlined under "Incremental Improvement" can also be implemented as a part of this effort. The difference is that in the "Metamorphosis" approach, there should be a much-enhanced level of support from leadership and hopefully a broader understanding of the mission and objectives across the organization.

Incremental Improvement [Taking what they give]

Vision

The Vision for the "Incremental" approach to information quality is very similar to the "Metamorphosis" path. The incremental approach deals with the scenario where executive leadership is at an earlier stage of maturity concerning the value of information. The assumption is that they will be less supportive of the changes required to become an information-centric enterprise, and this path will take much longer. It will require negotiation skills, political agility, patience, and perseverance.

Projects will also use the strategies for Incremental Improvement as a part of the Metamorphosis approach. In modern businesses, project teams must demonstrate incremental value to establish and maintain momentum and vitality, regardless of executive leadership's initial level of support.

The approach outlined here attempts to cope with the scenario where executive leadership has decided they want a data-driven enterprise, unencumbered by knowledge. This situation is usually the result of attending a conference or reading some articles and suddenly wanting to be able to say that the enterprise is "data-driven." "Make it so" leaders are both a blessing and a curse because they empower their resources to get some things done in some infrequent instances. However, far too often, they have unrealistic expectations and make demands unfettered by facts. In fairness, they are dealing with a wide variety of challenges and do need to delegate. However, in many cases, they are tempted by the bright and shiny allure of rapid faux delivery of results and sacrifice actual strategic value for the enterprise on the altar of an impressive quarterly report. Moreover, the fact that there is no mechanism to account for and track the accumulation of technical debt means they are not held accountable and are often not even aware of the magnitude of the mess they have created.

So, any professional dropped into this scenario and tasked with "fixing everything" is doomed to fail if they try to push the approach outlined under "Metamorphosis." Facts and logic do not matter in this scenario. Perception trumps reality, and the priority here needs to be survival and incremental improvement. This approach is about small wins, developing allies in the development and project communities, and hopefully cultivating a fanbase among executive leadership.

Strategies

Deliver Value Quickly and in Steady Increments

One of the factors that contributed to the failure of large-scale "Enterprise Data Model" efforts in the eighties and nineties was a tendency for the data architecture teams to try to "boil the ocean." They tried to model the entire enterprise completely before ever engaging with the development teams to provide value.

Data architecture during this period seemed to be a magnet for the "navel gazers" in the organization. These folks wanted to debate minute details about meta-concepts and theories endlessly. As a result, the most common response when I engaged with the project teams was that data architecture was an "ivory tower" or "academic" exercise. The project teams would state that they didn't have time to waste gathering definitions for the data elements they would be manipulating because they had code delivery milestones to meet.

Data architecture teams through this period spent months debating metadata modeling naming standards and guidelines, arguing over CASE tools, and configuring the environments.

Meanwhile, development and implementation projects were charging ahead, stacking up mountains of technical debt while the data architects dithered over class words and abbreviation standards. In the end, executive management looked at the enormous architectural plots on the walls and decided that the data architecture teams did not deliver enough value to continue funding them.

Modern I/T teams have learned to work with the concept of "Minimum Viable Product" [MVP] to shorten the time to Return on Investment [ROI]. It is vital to support this approach while increasing the value of the output from these efforts. The best way to do this is to anticipate what is next on the software developmental horizon and to get out and talk to the business. The goal is to define and model the information requirements that will fall within the scope of the upcoming development projects. As mentioned in "Root Cause," Agile needs to be enabled by having as solid a semantic foundation for the information elements in scope as possible to reduce rework and bugs.

Focus on Delivering Project-level Value

A large percentage of the development projects that get kicked off are working with thin (or non-existent) data dictionaries. Compound this with poorly named data attributes (because why bother making a variable name descriptive if it will take more typing?), and the data misery is absolute. To make matters more complicated, the frequent requirement to support a globally distributed development team has added international culture and language factors over the last few years as a consideration.

An exhaustive data dictionary is one of the most consistently well-received artifacts an information engineer can provide to a development team. The process of crafting plain business language descriptions for data elements is a rigorous one, and as a result, most developers enthusiastically avoid it. However, it remains vital that development teams, particularly large, globally distributed development teams, have consistent definitions to ensure that data is populated, processed, validated, and presented consistently and accurately.

Gently Evangelize Simplification

Dealing with these complicated application architectures, siloed data, and globally distributed resources is where some gentle pressure may be persuasive. A few well-placed questions can start the leadership and development teams to consider the value in reducing the number of "versions of truth" that siloed data stores create. Simply reducing the number and variety of interfaces to be managed is a significant addition of value to the enterprise.

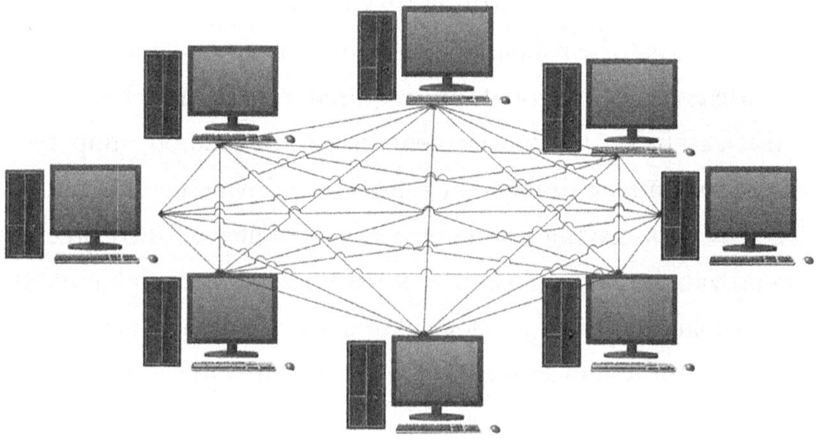

FIGURE 17 - POINT-TO-POINT INTERFACE COMPLEXITY

In the example illustrated above, for complete data sharing to occur across all eight of the constituent systems in the enterprise, a project team must implement and maintain 28 different interfaces. However, as can be seen in the following illustration, establishing a single "canonical" information hub can significantly reduce the number and complexity of interfaces in the environment while standardizing the data flowing through it and increasing the quality of the information derived from it.

Merely reducing the number of interfaces required is a significant accelerator to progress. However, the value in the "hub" end of the hub-and-spoke integration model having clearly worded, wholly described, and rigorously validated semantic descriptions for every attribute included cannot be over-stated. One of the most significant hindrances to progress in most integration efforts is that neither of the two systems involved has sufficiently precise descriptions for their data elements. So the first thing they must do is each system must figure out what their data is supposed to mean and then iron out any differences and negotiate any required transformations. Starting with at least half of the data elements clearly understood, jump-starts the process immeasurably. For integrations involving external service providers, having the enterprise's attributes defined precisely also provides an advantage in negotiating who needs to handle the transformations. Thus, it is logical to assert that the less clearly understood data system should transform to match the clearly defined data element.

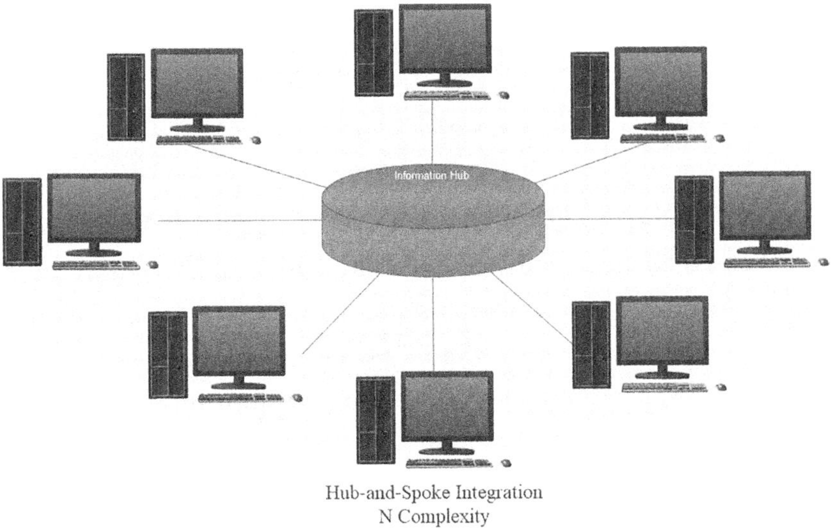

FIGURE 18 - INFORMATION HUB INTERFACE SIMPLIFICATION

As illustrated above, an "integration hub" can reduce the number of interfaces required to one per participating system (eight), thereby reducing the workload, simplifying the architecture to be supported, and speeding up the addition of new constituent systems.

Don't be narrow-minded about implementing the "Hub"

In looking at the preceding drawings, it is understandable to jump to the assumption that this implies some centralized data store. While implementing a canonical data store is certainly one approach to achieving this centralization, it is NOT the only approach. What is important is enabling the integration and reconciliation of "meaning" across all the diverse data storage solutions that have sprung up over time and continue to sprout at a breath-taking pace. Indeed, it is possible to implement a data services layer to accomplish much of the same function. Still, it is vital to ensure that all the data governance functionality is enabled to ensure consistency as the data flows across the system(s).

The Conceptual Information Model provides the roadmap/template to guide the edit/validation/governance requirements of the data services layer in question to achieve a de-coupling or abstraction of referencing the information content from the actual physical storage design.

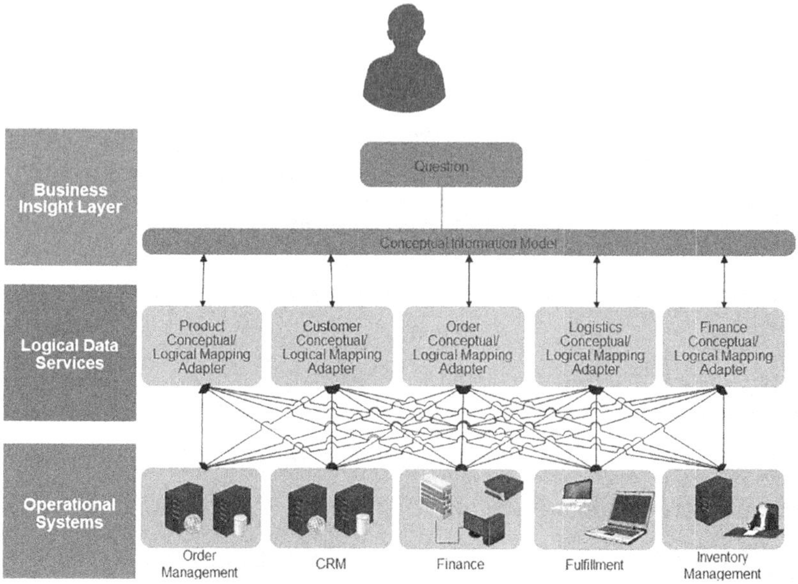

FIGURE 19 - INTEGRATION VIA SERVICES

Start with "Federation"

As an incremental approach to full-enterprise integration, it is possible to merely link key datasets from siloed repositories by establishing a "canonical" identity for the entities identified as part of the first pass. The candidates for these activities are usually some forms of "master data" that have broad usability/applicability across the enterprise. To be clear, the values in these federated systems may be collected to be displayed together. Still, there is no guarantee that analysts can create summaries until fully integrated to have the same meanings across systems. Nevertheless, the process of displaying them together can help identify the high-value first candidates for integration as funding is made available.

Build a "Proof of Concept" Integration Hub

Once the business SME has described a subject area within the Conceptual Information Model and the data architect models it to a satisfactory level of completeness, the designers can create a Logical Model in the desired target storage paradigm. The designers must be careful to maintain a 1:1 relationship with the Conceptual Information Model for the first pass and not prematurely "tune" the design.

Integrate as Requested and Funded

As the federated data and the limited set of integrated attributes begin to demonstrate value, there will be requests for additional capabilities. These should be collected, broken into subsets with functional or semantic affinity, and delivered as the business approves funding.

Establish Governance

Of course, the costs, resources, and staffing necessary to govern the growing collection of integrated data needs planning. At some point, leadership needs to formalize the official governance structure and empower roles. The hope is that this discussion happens after the value of reliable data/information has been thoroughly demonstrated.

It is not possible to exaggerate the necessity of governance because organizations tend toward entropy. Without a governing hand, development teams will opt for the "quicker" path to creating the data stores that they need rather than deal with the discipline required to utilize governed data sources.

Recognize the Contributors

Evangelizing for data quality and pushing to maintain it, while vital to an organization's long-term health and growth, is, at the same time, an incredibly thankless job.

Data quality advocates are not creating flashy dashboards or heat maps that excite executive leadership into frenzies of praise. Instead, they toil tirelessly in anonymity, reviewing descriptions, documentation, and pleading with management and executive to do "the right thing."

If not held up to the organization and praised for their efforts, the long-term results will be burned out data quality resources and increasing resistance from all who see data quality checks as a hindrance to speedy delivery.

Above all, sell, sell, sell

Marketing and promotion are natural skills to some. However, if you do not fall into that category, you will have to study the processes and learn them. Because without a steady drumbeat and a regular feed of instances where good quality data provided exceptional value to the enterprise, the voices of "hurry up and deliver" are going to win every time because they speak to the very core priorities of executive leadership… fast, measurable, delivery. Of course, that "delivery" may be flawed and may be adding corruption to the data stream, but that won't be obvious until months after credit for the "delivery" has been assigned.

Every new information capability needs to be recognized and praised; every new report enabled must be acknowledged; every new technology enabled must give credit to the high-quality data that allows it to function.

Suppose these beneficiaries do not maintain an awareness of and acknowledge the hard background work that happens upstream to enable their success? In that case, the data pipeline will become neglected, and results will degrade over time.

THE CONSULTING DATA OBSESSIVE [PT 2]

Mycroft Information Strategies

My welcome back to reality upon my return from my week working with Hec was the first strategy meeting of the NextGen Data Tiger Team.

My review of the accumulated emails showed that the corporate antibodies were already busily at work, determining how significant this initiative's threat was and positioning resources to deal with it.

The ERP group, who had been so busy that they could only offer up a single resource initially, now demanded that a representative from each of their functioning instances of the software have a seat in the team. Further, they notified us that their Senior Director, Allison Fassbinder, would attend the kickoff meeting to "set expectations." This last bit of news put me in an awkward position since Ms. Fassbinder outranked me in the organization by a couple of levels, but when I asked my boss, Ms. Carruthers, to attend as well, she begged off, claiming she was booked solid.

Perhaps I should mention at this point that this abandonment in the breach was not a big surprise. Because sadly, a few things had become apparent in the few weeks I had worked for Ms. Carruthers.

Ms. Carruthers had a faded beauty about her that hinted at a genuinely gifted youth. She had an effortless grace and a presumption of place in executive meetings, especially when the makeup of the gathering was predominantly male. She had risen rapidly through the organization by carefully noting which direction the winds of power were blowing and adjusting course to take advantage of them.

Her background was predominantly as a project manager for large software projects, and she had virtually no experience in data architecture, data quality, or data governance.

After the strategy of shifting Mycroft to a data-driven focus became a hot topic among executives, and when my boss resigned to take the CDO job, she quickly lobbied her way into being put in charge of the Data Services Group. However, I noticed that she called the team together for even the most minor of strategy decisions, never contributed any actual content to the discussions, and never took the visible lead on anything that might become contentious. As a result, I was uneasy about the level of support I could expect if the NextGen Data team encountered headwinds.

In addition to the ERP group's newly discovered enthusiasm about data, the corporate Project Management Office also demanded a representative in the group. I was a little embarrassed that they hadn't been on Ms. Carruthers' original invitation because I knew that their buy-in and support would be critical to our long-term success, so I hastily added them to the meeting invitation.

I was glad that MJ had scheduled the meeting as a virtually hosted event because if we had been having a face-to-face meeting, I'd have been looking for a larger meeting room since the original attendee list had more than doubled.

A small part of me was excited to be leading a group that was generating such interest. However, a more significant part of me was concerned about the variety of perspectives and agendas represented in what was supposed to be an initial kick-off meeting.

I decided to add a detailed agenda to the meeting invitation, which Ms. Carruthers had initially sent out with just a title of 'NextGen Data Tiger Team Kickoff.' We needed focus in this initial discussion, or things were going to get out of hand quickly. We could schedule follow-on meetings for specific concerns and issues while getting our initial discussion covered.

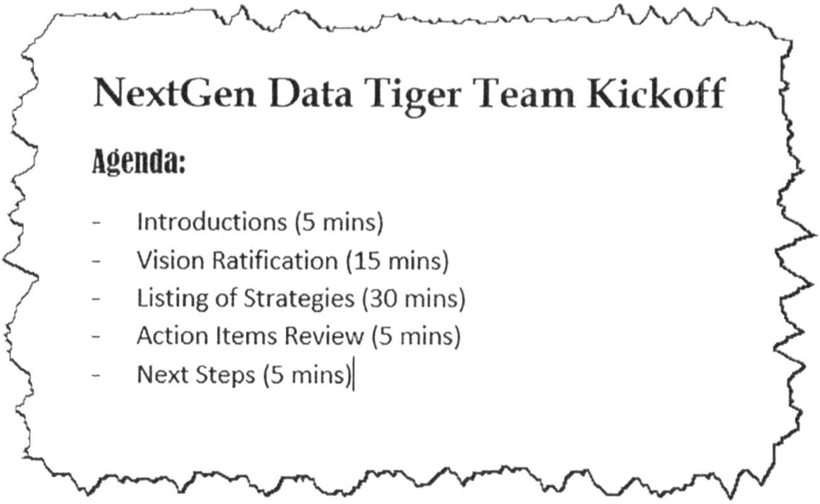

NextGen Data Tiger Team Kickoff

Agenda:

- Introductions (5 mins)
- Vision Ratification (15 mins)
- Listing of Strategies (30 mins)
- Action Items Review (5 mins)
- Next Steps (5 mins)

FIGURE 20 - NEXTGEN KICKOFF AGENDA

The final newly added attendee to the meeting who promised to provide some of the biggest challenges was Jonathan Fogbottom, the Executive VP of Enterprise Data.

Mr. Fogbottom had written a book called "Enterprise Data Done Right" about seven years ago. The CEO at the time had been so impressed with it that he had immediately rushed out and brought Mr. Fogbottom into the organization as a senior executive to fix all the data issues at Mycroft.

Armed with the authority of the CEO, Mr. Fogbottom had established the "Enterprise Data Group." He then set about scheduling countless planning sessions and forming working groups to develop data standards. These standards focused on data modeling standards, including naming conventions and abbreviations while imposing a draconian level of data compliance checkpoints on software development projects. The data requirements documentation load was so burdensome that software delivery ground to a virtual halt as they worked through the massive level of documentation and metadata requirements demanded by the new data regime.

Eventually, the project teams used the realities of a fast-paced business climate to get exceptions authorized. Once the project teams had identified the 'patterns of avoidance' for Enterprise Data standards, they effectively used them. As a result, virtually every project that came through had one of the mitigating factors that allowed them to bypass the Enterprise Data standards requirements.

It was not lost on anyone, least of all Mr. Fogbottom, that when executive leadership decided to stand up the NextGen Data Services Team, they put the team under someone else's control. The stated reason was that this effort focused more on the actual utilization of the data than its pure architecture. However, the reality was that the executives intended for NextGen to develop something leaner that would still provide necessary data quality.

Ms. Carruthers' thinking when she opted not to invite Mr. Fogbottom to the kickoff meeting is subject to speculation. It could have been just an oversight, or she could have wanted to avoid distractions, but whatever her reason, Mr. Fogbottom had discovered the meeting was being held and demanded an invitation.

As would be expected, Ms. Carruthers apologized for the oversight, and by her repeated mention of my name in her email response, obviously intended to imply that the faux pas had been mine. And tellingly, she closed the email with a rather pointed instruction for me to update the meeting invitation to include Mr. Fogbottom.

While the project teams had pulled most of the teeth from the Enterprise Data group and exposed Mr. Fogbottom's lack of real authority, he still had a senior executive-level position, and Ms. Carruthers wasn't taking any chances.

This meeting was going to be a challenge.

Kick-off Meeting

Five minutes before the scheduled start time for the meeting, I fired up the virtual meeting environment and settled in. Then, one by one, the attendees showed up on the screen, exchanged pleasantries, and we all waited for the few stragglers to join.

I started the meeting by introducing myself, providing a quick overview of what we would discuss, sharing the meeting agenda, noting how tight the schedule was, and asking everyone to introduce themselves. Most of the participants had worked together on previous projects, so the introductions went pretty quickly.

With the introductions completed, I said, "This is the list of desired supported capabilities that Ms. Carruthers provided as a starting point. Does anyone have anything to add, any questions, or any modifications to suggest?" and shared the following on the screen:

- Predictive Analytics
- Machine Learning
- Artificial Intelligence
- Internet of Things connectivity
- Full-Sale-Cycle Real-Time Dashboard
- Global Real-Time Supply Chain monitoring
- Blockchain-enabled contracts
- streamlined regulatory compliance
- flexible future-proofed architecture

"Excuse me, Mr. Swan, but before we get into the details of this, I'd like to get some clarification on who has sign-off authority for the policies, standards, and procedures that come out of this group." Mr. Fogbottom interjected.

"Jon, we've discussed this and in the last Executive Steering Committee meeting…." Ms. Carruthers began. The conversation lasted for the next 45 minutes, with Mr. Fogbottom strenuously asserting that anything about data was the domain of the Enterprise Data group. Ms. Carruthers would counter, trying to resist and retain control of her new group without saying anything that Mr. Fogbottome could use against her with the executive steering committee.

Finally, Ms. Carruthers said, "Well, Jon, I don't think we are going to be able to resolve this today, perhaps we'd better table this discussion, and I'll schedule a follow-up with the Executive Steering Committee."

"I think that would be a good idea, Ms. Carruthers; I look forward to that conversation," replied Mr. Fogbottom.

"Well, it looks like we have pretty well run out of time, so I'll look into rescheduling this kickoff meeting after you folks have resolved the reporting issues, shall I?" I offered.

Everyone nodded in agreement, so I said, "Okay, you folks have a great day!" and I ended the meeting.

I sighed and put my face in my hands.

Adjustments

MJ must have initially felt like she had pretty strong support from the Executive Steering Committee because she quickly scheduled a meeting to discuss Mr. Fogbottom's concerns for the following week.

Meanwhile, MJ and I had a quick debrief following the failed kickoff meeting. In an attempt to continue moving forward, MJ and I agreed that a smaller targeted group of individuals would get together to do an initial draft of a vision statement that the larger group could then ratify. MJ tasked me with scheduling that meeting and delivering the first draft of the vision statement.

Vision Working Session

I invited Ahmso Greene (since she was still the only representative the business had designated), John Clay, and Duncan Ross to the working session. I thought that we'd have the business, I/T, and the ERP systems represented if any questions arose about the provenance of the vision statement. Since the entire team would review and edit it, I felt like we had good coverage but wanted to avoid any obvious hurdles if possible.

I was able to find a one-hour slot early in the day on all of their calendars for the next day, so I scheduled the virtual meeting and was pleasantly surprised to get reasonably quick acceptances from all invitees. I had a sneaking suspicion that some of them just wanted follow-up inside information on the scuffle between MJ and Mr. Fogbottom. Still, I would take their participation however I could get it.

Sure enough, no sooner had we all joined than Ahmso asked, "So… any updates on Fogbottom vs. Carruthers – the Battle Near the Cattle? [referencing our proximity to the Ft Worth stockyards] Do we have a winner, or will there be more rounds to come?" I tried to smile noncommittally and updated them that the discussion with the executives would be happening the following week.

"In the interim," I continued, "I thought that it made sense for us to try to come up with a draft vision statement. Then, the broader group can refine it rather than try to distill a common thread from a dozen different perspectives at the same time."

Everyone nodded, so I continued. "We've seen the list of features, technologies, and characteristics that leadership intends for MORIARTI to enable, but I think we need to reshape that into a more cohesive vision statement. Does anyone have any thoughts?"

Duncan Ross offered, "Well, should we mention how critical it is that we support Copper Beeches? It is, after all, our main software environment and kind of the big dog in the room."

"Software comes and goes, and I think it is important that we keep the vision statement very conceptual and not include any current technologies or brand names. The intent is for the vision to guide our strategies for an extended period if we get it right", I said. "I think that a reference to core business data should cover that space adequately, don't you?" Duncan nodded.

John Clay chimed in with, "Well, actually MORIARTI is primarily going to be a data conduit for all of those capabilities, so perhaps we focus on the data-related capabilities and qualities that MORIARTI is to provide?"

"I think that makes sense... I have a list that I wrote down on my little shadowing adventure at Baker, and they permitted me to reuse it; let me find it in my notes," I said as I searched for the file in my archive.

I pulled up the list of Information Qualities that we had come up with and asked, "How does this look as a starting point?"

Understandability - Each data element should be exhaustively and unambiguously defined to ensure proper usage and interpretation.

Accuracy - Each data element should have processes in place to ensure that the values contained therein are correct and current.

Flexibility - Data structures should be built in such a way as to facilitate reuse across existing systems as well as being able to rapidly adapt to support future requirements.

Usefulness - Data collected and maintained should be suitable for and have value to a business usage by the enterprise.

Reliability - Data stores should be structured to ensure they remain available.

Accessibility - Data should be maintained in such a way that all interested parties can get to it.

Security - Data should be protected to ensure that only legitimate users are able to access it.

Comprehensiveness - Efforts should be made to ensure that all of the required data needed by the business is available.

FIGURE 21 - INFORMATION QUALITIES FROM BAKER

"I think those are a handy reference," John Clay offered, "we just need to come up with a brief cohesive statement that reflects those qualities and provides us with a clear enough destination that we can know when we've wandered 'off course.'"

"Agreed," I replied, "The main purpose for the vision is to set a destination for us to use as a reference point for evolving strategies."

"So," John began, "How about 'MORIARTI will speed access to all data within Mycroft and improve availability.'?"

"That's a good start," I offered, "...however if you don't improve data quality, aren't you just enabling more people to make bad decisions faster?"

John winced, "Well, everyone knows data quality is in there.".

"And that is the problem," I said. "Everyone assumes that someone else is taking responsibility, and it is such an ugly job that no one wants to take it on. However, speedy access and availability are key features, and this is a good start."

"How about we amend it to read, 'MORIARTI will speed access to all data within Mycroft and improve the availability of reliable information to assist in making sound decisions.'? We can then reference the list of qualities to define further what we mean by 'reliable,'" John offered.

"But 'reliability' is one of the qualities listed," Ahmso pointed out.

"Sure," John said, "But if you look at the definition, I think that we can substitute 'availability', and we are good to go."

"Fair enough," Duncan offered, "but I think that we need to explicitly call out security, even though we include it as one of our traits of reliability."

"I agree," John countered, "How about we amend it to read, 'MORIARTI will speed access to all data within Mycroft and improve the availability of reliable information to assist in making sound decisions while managing and securing the data as a valuable resource.'?"

"There's just one little problem." I offered, "An ideal vision statement is seven words plus or minus two. We aren't writing a whitepaper or a technical spec, so we need to be pithy."

"How about 'Secure, reliable, faster data… now'?" I offered.

There was a brief pause while the rest of the attendees considered the idea. Slowly they all began to nod their heads, and I asked, "So is this it? Are we happy with this?" and received pleased nods from everyone.

"Alright, I'll present this as our draft vision for MORIARTI at the next attempted Kick-off meeting," I said and received chuckles in return.

"Is there anything else that we should discuss before ending the call?" I asked.

John Clay said, "Just one idea that I'd like to throw out there for consideration. We've watched the 'Big Bang' approach to data quality struggle for the last few years now, and I think that indicates that we need to consider a different approach."

"Okay," I replied, "I'm certainly interested in anything that will increase our chances of a successful outcome."

"Well," John continued, "I don't think that the organization is going to be open to a whole new set of standards, procedures, and checkpoints in the interest of improving data quality, so I think that we take a 'Crawl/Walk/Run' approach."

In response to Duncan's audible groan, John said, "No, now hear me out… I know that there is a lot of bad press out there on Crawl/Walk/Run as a strategy, and it has become a bit of a meme, but even if we don't label it as such, it might be the way that we get our foot in the door and demonstrate some momentum before putting too great a burden on the project teams."

Despite my doubts, in the interest of maintaining a teaming spirit, I agreed to bring it up as one of the strategies for consideration when we got to that point.

"If that's all, then I'll talk to you folks at the Kick-off meeting!" I concluded and ended the call.

Surrender

I received a call that afternoon from MJ informing me that she had decided that it wasn't worth the fuss of getting the executives involved. So instead, I was to include Mr. Fogbottom in all emails and meeting invitations in the future.

I pointed out that Mr. Fogbottom had created many of the problems that we were trying to address. In addition, his involvement as a gatekeeper would exponentially complicate getting anything done. MJ sniffed and said, "If you don't think you are up to the challenge, I can find someone else." As things played out, I came to dearly wish that I'd just said "Fine" at that point, but my ego and professional pride got in the way of my better judgment, and I said, "No, I'll find a way to work around it."

I learned later via the grapevine that after her momentary bravado in the kickoff meeting, she had become anxious about standing up to Mr. Fogbottom and had chosen to give in and keep him informed on our activities rather than force the issue. But, sadly, this was not the last time she would abandon the NextGen Data team in a crisis.

Kickoff Redux

I scheduled the second attempt at a kickoff meeting with diminished enthusiasm. I knew that the surrender to Mr. Fogbottom would signal to all the interested parties that this was a toothless Tiger Team and make our negotiations even more difficult in the future.

Specifically, the issues that I already knew we were going to face, by group, were:

I/T – The Agile teams would object on principle to anything that they perceived as additional documentation. If they gave ground on the value of the data dictionary, there would be a battle over what constituted a "good" definition.

Additionally, there was an almost religious belief that there had to be a technological solution to data quality. The only reason I/T hadn't solved it was that they just hadn't purchased the right software yet.

Business – The business didn't want to be bothered. The business viewed data quality as an I/T issue, and no one dared to challenge it when the business claimed that SMEs didn't have time to get involved in software projects. They typically (as in this case) sent their least valuable resources, claiming that all their senior resources were too busy.

Copper Beeches ERP teams – The ERP folks resisted/objected to getting engaged in defining their data fundamentally out of honest ignorance of how tremendously useless the definitions in their software were. However, that didn't stop them from presenting their objections with a massive dose of arrogant condescension that anyone would dare question those definitions. They were also paranoid that the process would reveal that they had done full ERP implementations without a thoroughly documented understanding of the business they were trying to automate. Finally, they were terrified that the revelation might diminish their presumed unassailable leverage within the company.

And now, to make the situation worse, we were required to negotiate with an executive whose entire reason for being with the company was being questioned. His methodology, which he considered his life's work, was being called into question, and I expected him to be defensive.

Nope, I was not looking forward to this meeting at all.

Applying lessons learned from the first kickoff meeting, I pared the schedule down to two items: vision ratification and role clarification. Again, based on the first meeting, I was unsure that we could get that accomplished in an hour, but we had to start somewhere.

I sent the invitations to all of the previous meeting's attendees and had received acceptance notifications from everyone in reasonably short order.

Small Victories

When the time came, one by one, everyone logged into the meeting, and the customary greetings and chit-chat ensued.

When everyone had joined, I opened the meeting with "Good morning, folks! We are here for the second kickoff meeting for the NextGen Data Tiger Team, and I appreciate all of you making time to be here!"

"There were some organizational issues surfaced in the last meeting that Mr. Fogbottom and Ms. Carruthers worked out, so here we are once again!"

"One of the stated goals of the charter of the Tiger Team is to find a way to improve the quality and management of our data. So we are going to be pursuing some creative strategies to do that. However, before we begin discussing 'how' we will get a good result, it is important to have a clear description of what that destination is to know when our journey may have veered off-course. That description is captured in a vision statement, and a few of us met in a working group and created a draft vision statement for review, comment, and modification by the broader team."

With that, I shared the vision statement on the screen: "Secure, reliable, faster data... now."

I was a bit surprised when the reaction was primarily thoughtful acceptance, one or two expressions of grudging indifference, and more than a couple of indications of relief that I assume had to do with not having to work through this process.

After a minute or two had passed, I asked, "Do we agree to this as our Vision for MORIARTI?"

There were general murmurs of assent and head nods, so I said, "Great! Let's move on to roles!"

The following 20 minutes involved a back and forth over RACI charts, with Mr. Fogbottom demanding to be consulted on every action and eventually accepting the promise of being informed since that was all that his tussle with Ms. Carruthers had yielded.

With the vision and roles reasonably fixed, I was about to adjourn the meeting when Mr. Fogbottom interjected, "I can provide the list of data architecture artifacts currently specified by the Enterprise Data team for everyone to review before our next meeting if you'd like."

I inwardly cringed because I knew that the Agile advocates would not welcome this. Mr. Fogbottom's definition of a minimum data documentation set had been the cause of many pitched battles over the last five years.

Mr. Fogbottom's perspective on requirements documentation was firmly rooted in traditional waterfall development methodologies. Before any coding activities could start in these waterfall methodologies, a requirements team would produce a comprehensive set of requirements and design documents. As such, he expected a conceptual information model, a logical data model, and a CRUD matrix to be provided as milestone deliverables to get out of the design phase of a project.

The reality was that project teams had become masters of avoiding complying with the Enterprise Data Architecture group's standards. Instead, they would find exceptions for their projects to get them "fast-tracked" by the PMO outside of the "standard" development process requirements, and so for the most part, they ignored Mr. Fogbottom's expectations.

It turned out that the MORIARTI project had performed the same maneuver, and it had been designated as "mission-critical R&D," so we were free to define our process and milestones as long as we filed it with the PMO and got it approved.

"Thank you, Mr. Fogbottom," I replied, "Please do send a copy of those to me, and I'll get them saved into our project archive so they are available when we have our first strategy and process meeting next week. As you know, we are running this project under an exception, so we will need to agree on exactly the documentation requirements for this process. Still, it is always nice to be able to leverage previous efforts."

His expression was a strange combination of satisfaction and anxiety as he said, "Very well; I'll send them along."

Mine-field Pig

I scheduled the first Strategy planning session for MORIARTI. I was fretting about the battle that I KNEW would ensue when Mr. Fogbottom started pushing for his lengthy list of data artifacts as minimum requirements. But then, a new thought dawned on me.

I only really wanted solid data element definitions as the minimum data documentation for the requirements milestone. I knew that I would get pushback from the Agile team if I went in and pushed for that initially. However, suppose I let Mr. Fogbottom go in and demand his suite of artifacts and let them wear each other down for a while. In that case, I could then come in and offer my data element definitions as a "compromise" and have a much better chance of getting the Agile team to agree. The fact is that they all knew that the definitions would be helpful to them. Hence, their argument about "needless documentation" was half-hearted at best. This way, they could get out of there without having the hefty modeling requirements that Mr. Fogbottom wanted to add.

I confess that I chuckled a little as I hit the send key on the meeting invitation. "Mr. Fogbottom may not be such a bad addition to the mix after all," I thought.

Crawl/Walk/Run

When the first strategy meeting rolled around, I was anxious because we needed to make some headway. However, based on the personalities and agendas invited to this call, there were a variety of different ways the wheels could come off this meeting.

But I fired up the virtual meeting and greeted everyone as they joined with a big smile. Once everyone had joined, I started with, "Okay, I guess one of the first things we need to agree upon is what the bare minimum list of data artifacts are that we are going to require to allow a project to proceed into development. Bear in mind that what is being collected currently by the non-Enterprise-Data-standards -following projects is inadequate. Otherwise, we wouldn't be here, so without creating unnecessary work and delay, what are the bare minimums that we need?"

Mr. Fogbottom leaped into the discussion with enthusiasm and conviction, "The current list of artifacts is exceptionally lean, and I think entirely reasonable as a minimum set of requirements for any serious …"

"You've got to be kidding me!" interrupted Gerta Klacken, Senior Scrum Master and spokesperson for the Agile project teams. Gerta wasn't known for her winning personality, but she had a track record for driving her teams to deliver software on time, so management gave her a relatively large amount of leeway. "We don't have time to spend hours interviewing business people and drawing data models that no one will ever use! We're far better off getting the screens in front of people and adjusting things as needed."

"But we've established that incrementally evolving screens and processes can work, but missing data requirements is much more costly in rework and …" Mr. Fogbottom began, and they were off.

As much as I knew that we needed to make progress in this meeting, I also knew that I needed to let them blow off some of this energy and get tired of the struggle before I waded into the fray. Otherwise, I'd get drawn into taking sides, and that wasn't going to get us anywhere productive.

So, I let them go back and forth for about ten minutes or so before I stepped in. Then, finally, I started, "Look, we need something additional going into the first sprint on these projects because what we are coming out the back end with currently is almost unmaintainable. It is poorly understood, hard to use, and in many cases, the data is of extremely low quality. So, what is a reasonable minimum data artifact list upon which we can agree?"

Allison Fassbinder, the Senior Director of ERP Systems, who I was a bit surprised to see joining this call, spoke up, "If I may offer a suggestion, to get some momentum, might we pursue a 'Crawl/Walk/Run' sort of an approach?"

"Hmmm… Crawl/Walk/Run again," I thought as I glanced at John Clay. He appeared a little uneasy, and I smelled a setup.

"What do you mean?" I replied.

"Well, how about initially we just start by requiring a set of completed definitions for all data elements in the scope of the project before the start of the first sprint?" she offered.

"We work with that requirement for a few projects, and then as teams get comfortable with that as a deliverable, we can add other artifacts as we identify them as being needed. That way, we don't overwhelm the Agile teams with a new large packet of deliverables, and they can get accustomed to the new way of doing things."

On its face, I didn't have any objections to Ms. Fassbender's proposal, and indeed, a data dictionary was my target "get" for this meeting. However, I was still uneasy with why she showed up to this meeting and was so helpful.

However, feeling like I needed to take "yes" as an answer, I decided to play along. "Well, that sounds like a reasonable approach to me. Does anyone else object?"

And of course, Mr. Fogbottom had to object, but it was apparent that he had figured out that this battle was over, and before long, he relented. We agreed that our "Crawl"-level Data Requirements milestone deliverable would be a Data Dictionary.

With that, we adjourned the meeting, and I tried to feel like we had made some good progress but was still unable to shake a nagging sense of foreboding.

"Win Friends and Influence People"

Being right is not enough.

As we worked to get as many modeling and data description artifacts collected to include in our integrated model, we were made aware of a model developed previously and which had gained a bit of traction among parts of the business. Executive leadership felt that incorporating this model and knowledge base into our environment would encourage the model's fans to embrace our approach. Hence, MJ instructed us to get with the original architect in charge of the model, Richard Boca, and see what we could work out. However, MJ warned us that while Richard had significant knowledge of the system and data in question, the consensus was that Richard was "difficult to work with."

If anything, MJ understated the warning. Richard managed to hold his tongue for the first few minutes of the meeting, but it was apparent that he was frustrated. When he finally did start talking, the message communicated was that we were all simple-minded and that efforts to create an enterprise information model had failed before and that we would all fail just like the previous efforts had. Richard made it clear that he felt that the reference data model and architecture that he had created was far superior to anything we could imagine and that we should just use that model and work from that. Not having been given access to the model yet, I focused on establishing a relationship, building lines of communication, and getting access to the documentation.

Unfortunately, there was a much larger audience for this meeting, and it included executive sponsors and business SMEs that came away from the meeting convinced that Richard was a problem. Subsequently, they moved Richard away from the project. However, before leaving, a few weeks later, I did receive the documentation and model for the data repository in question.

I still vividly remember the growing sense of shock that came over me as I went through the documentation. It was some of the most beautiful work I had ever seen, and I could see why Richard was so proud of it and convinced of its value. The problem was, he had so poisoned the well in his interactions with previous development teams and SMEs that I/T and the business had stopped listening and finally just moved the perceived problem out of the way.

Even though Richard had been infuriating to deal with, I was still sorry to see someone marginalized and moved off who had done this level of quality work. It was a bit of a teachable moment for me.

Mycroft Struggles to Perform

Crawl/Walk/Run Revealed

Over the next few months, it became clear that by "Crawl/Walk/Run," Ms. Fassbinder had really meant "Crawl/Stall/Fail."

The time came for the initial data requirements checkpoint review for the first Copper Beeches-related project to go through the new process. Two weeks before the scheduled sign-off, the project team submitted their requirements artifacts without a data dictionary. Despite multiple emails requesting the data dictionary, we had received no responses. When asked why the project team had neglected to include the data dictionary deliverable in the sign-off packet, the answer was, "Oh, the definitions for all those elements are in the base install of Copper Beeches, so we're good." When asked to see the definitions, the team responded, "They are all readily available in the online tool." When asked to pull up the in-scope descriptions in the online tool, they claimed to not know right off hand where to find the definitions but that they'd get back to us and provide that information "if we just had to have it."

They were aghast when I informed them that they would not be getting a sign-off for their project to proceed. The project team railed about how dogmatic we were and how silly it was to derail the project's progress over something trivial as this, and that the definitions were all in the tool. It was Copper Beeches, after all!

When it became clear that the data review team wasn't going to relent, the Copper Beeches project lead assured me that we'd be hearing from Ms. Fassbinder shortly.

I did not doubt that.

Two hours later, my telephone rang, and the caller ID said it was "A. Fassbinder." She said that she'd heard from her project lead that the NextGen Data team was being unreasonable. When I reminded her that the minimum agreed-upon deliverable for the data checkpoint was a data dictionary, she said, "But all those definitions are already in Copper Beeches," to which I replied, "And we are just asking to review them for completeness." She followed up with, "Are you questioning the quality of our work with the Copper Beeches implementation?". I sighed inwardly, seeing where this one was going. "I do not have enough information to do such a thing. I do not have enough information to form an opinion either way. I am responsible for ensuring that we clearly understand and have documented the data adequately before development proceeds. That is all I am trying to evaluate."

"Well, we can't have this project delayed over clerical paper shuffling. I'll contact MJ and get this straightened out." Ms. Fassbinder replied as she hung up the phone.

It was about this time that it dawned on me why Ms. Fassbinder had so eagerly pushed for the data dictionary to be the "Crawl" level data deliverable. She believed that the default definitions in the Copper Beeches package would be sufficient to bypass the checkpoint. Apparently, her team members had a better idea of just how weak and ambiguous the default definitions were and were now dragging their feet about giving us visibility to those definitions.

The problem is that the package's definitions were intentionally brief and ambiguous to allow the software to apply to as many customers as possible. The intent was that the customers could update the descriptions to be more precise and rigorous once installed and configured. Sadly, this last step rarely happened and certainly had not happened for any of the Mycroft instances of Copper Beeches.

About an hour later, MJ called, and her tone was frosty. "Well, I just had a lovely chat with Allison Fassbinder, and she isn't happy. So what is the issue with the Copper Beeches project sign-off?"

I reminded MJ of what we had agreed to as a deliverable for the data requirements sign-off. I described how the Copper Beeches team had shown up to the sign-off, having provided no data dictionary for the in-scope data elements despite repeated requests.

"Well, we can't hold up the project on a technicality, so I'm going to issue an exemption and let them proceed," MJ said.

"Ms. Carruthers, if you do that… If we surrender the very first time there is pushback on our minimal attempt to make things better, we will never get anything turned around," I said.

"Well, JT, what do you want me to do? Just not let any project pass the checkpoint without definitions?" she asked, and the smirk in her tone was unmistakable.

"Yes," I replied.

"Well, you don't understand the bigger picture, JT. We have a business to run, and we can't be petty about small details," she answered.

"Ms. Carruthers, we are the 'NextGen Data' team, and data quality is the heart of what we do. The definition of a data element drives the design, population, modification, validation, and consumption of that data element. I wouldn't call that a small detail. However, you are the Director of Data Services, and this is your call."

We hung up the phone, and I stared out the window, feeling my pulse in my temple.

Agile Push-Back

After I left work, I couldn't stop replaying the conversation with MJ in my head. I rehashed it thru dinner and several times as I tried to unwind with my guitar. I was usually able to lose myself in music, but tonight work just kept forcing its way back to the front of my mind. Concern about how I'd care for my mom if I lost my job nagged at me incessantly. Finally, I managed to sleep and arrived at work the next day, tired and dreading the next project information requirements review scheduled for mid-morning.

This scheduled project review was an Agile team that had submitted a document that they called their data definitions. The first review of the artifact revealed unacceptably brief data attribute descriptions and extremely short (ambiguous) attribute naming. The document had been sent back within a day with explanations. The expectation was that it would be updated and resubmitted. When the project team did not resubmit the artifact within a couple of days, we followed up in an attempt to make sure that it was finalized in time for the review and were told, "We're working on it." So, we waited.

The afternoon before the review (just before I met with MJ), the email had arrived with their "revisions." They had made half-hearted attempts at improving the naming and added some text to their definitions, which in many cases had prompted more questions.

As we started the meeting, Harold Nuckless, the lead developer for the Dev team, said, "Gerta was running late and said she'd try to get here for the second half of the meeting."

"Very good; let's get started then," I replied. "I've still got some questions about some of these definitions you provided, and we need to get them resolved before signing off to proceed into development," I said.

"Why is that, JT?" Harry asked, "I thought they made sense to me, and we need to be focusing on project startup tasks. All these definitions take a lot of time, and we don't know the answers to a lot of your questions".

"I sympathize, Harry because I know how much work goes into good definitions. And I also know that many of the questions I asked were related to business concepts in the terms. But every one of those questions I asked represents a potential bug in the system if a developer makes an incorrect assumption about the meaning. It will be much easier to incorporate the answer before a lot of code is built on top of it than to change it after starting development. Agile streamlines evolving process (code) and user interface changes. However, underlying data changes are still a problem for Agile, and anything that we can catch before design and coding begins is a huge boost to productivity."

Harry sighed but said, "I suppose that makes sense. But how long do you think it will take us to get the definitions solid enough to proceed?"

"I'll see if I can get time with an SME next week, and we can probably get the remaining issues ironed out and be ready for sign-off after that," I said.

"Okay, I guess that will work," Harry replied.

About this time, Gerta swirled into the room with much huffing and sighing and took her place at the table as she not-so-gently plopped her worn backpack down. "So, are we all signed off and ready to go?" she asked.

"Well, we have a few more questions to get resolved on some of the definitions and …".

"What!?" Gerta spluttered. "You have GOT to be kidding me! We submitted the updated definitions yesterday, and we don't have any more time to waste on this silliness."

"Gerta, we talked about it, and ..." Harry started.

"No, I don't care what you talked about. We need to get started coding because there's going to be a lot of debugging later; there always is." She said as her hand slapped the top of the table. "I'm going to escalate this to MJ... This delay is just unacceptable!"

"Okay, Gerta, we had a plan in place to work through the remaining issues, but ..." I started.

"No, we've just got to get this resolved. We cannot be 'faster, better, cheaper' if we keep putting these roadblocks to progress in place," Gerta interrupted. The Senior Vice President of Operations said just last week that 'Speed trumps everything' and that is the guiding principle that we are going to follow."

I confess I was frustrated after two interruptions to our attempted explanations to her, so I probably engaged more directly than I should have. "Well, I guess that all comes back to 'definitions,' Gerta, as in what your definition of 'progress' is. If your definition of progress is rushing out and slinging some ill-defined code into production and making some lights blink on a screen, and declaring success, then yes, we want to be a roadblock to that. And if you plan to rush to something else before the awful quality of the data you are pumping can be discovered, then yes, we truly do want to be a roadblock to that kind of progress."

"However, if your definition of success includes providing immediate and lasting value to the enterprise while enabling future innovations and opening up the possibility of new insights to executive leadership, then no, we are not creating roadblocks."

"I do not know why it is so hard for you to see that solid definitions speed up your development process at almost every single phase after requirements."

"Oh really..." she sneered.

"Yes, really," I interrupted her and continued. "You have a team of about 12 different developers working locally in this facility. That's twelve different potential cultures, languages, types of upbringings, and educations that all have to somehow come to the same understanding of between 400 and 500 data attributes to develop an application that consistently manipulates those data attributes. But you somehow think that can happen with the sketchy ambiguous fluff that you pitched over the wall to get a box checked. Well, my job is to see to it that we improve the quality of the data that we move around our systems, and the first step of that is ensuring that the definitions are useful, and that's what I intend to do."

"In addition to your local developers, you have a team of about 24 remote developers with a completely different social, linguistic, and educational heritage. Are you going to sit there and tell me that you think that they are going to miraculously come to the same precise understanding of all 400 to 500 data attributes as your local team does without some guidance?"

"Well, they can always call..." she started.

"They are offset schedule-wise by 12 hours from us, and any question that has to be answered by us incurs a 24-hour delay at a minimum. Therefore, wouldn't it make more sense to anticipate some of the questions and build the answers into a reference that could allow them to proceed in a useful manner?"

"And to be clear, each and every single attribute in the information catalog gets 'defined' before it gets used. So every single time a developer figures out what an attribute is and how to use it, they are 'defining' it for themselves if no standard definition is available. So doesn't it make more sense to go through the process of determining the precise definitions one time with business SMEs validating the result and writing those definitions down to be reused over, and over, and over... Every single time someone uses one of the data elements?"

"But it's about more than just what is in it for the developers, even though I know that is your primary concern. From the enterprise perspective, capturing rigorous definitions will speed up the testing process and the ultimate rollout of the application. Ultimately, solid descriptions will infinitely increase the usability of the data when it finally is captured and made available to future business analysts, reporting analysts, system integrators, data scientists, and artificial intelligence instances."

"So Gerta, if you want to escalate this one, please do so. Because this is the hill I will defend, and I think I can make a pretty compelling case that rigorous definitions are not a luxury and that the ask is entirely reasonable," I concluded.

Harry sat uncomfortably to the side during this exchange and kept his eyes firmly affixed on his notepad.

Gerta stared at me with narrowed eyes and pursed lips, considering her next move. I had no illusions about having persuaded her and felt sure that she was calculating her odds of coming out on top in a showdown in front of MJ. The fact that Gerta took as long to respond made me feel confident that she had not yet heard the story of the outcome of the previous afternoon's meeting with Ms. Fassbinder. Otherwise, Gerta would have been quicker to press the issue on MJ while MJ was on the defensive.

Gerta decided to get a better understanding of what leverage she had before pressing the matter further because she said, "You said you had a plan... just how much is this plan going to set us back timewise?"

Harry offered hopefully, "We are going to work through the remaining questions and be ready to go by the end of next week."

Gerta sniffed and said, "Well, I guess we can focus on platform and setup tasks while you get that finished off, but it cannot drag on past next Friday!"

"Okay, Gerta, we'll get it done," Harry promised.

"Okay then, well, I have another meeting to get to, so I'll talk to both of you next week," Greta said as she scooped up her backpack and swept out of the room.

I looked over at Harry and smiled and winked as I said, "Well, I think I'll have your full engagement on getting those definitions refined."

Harry was less amused.

Venting

At the end of a reasonably challenging week, I decided that it would be a bit of a relief to talk to Hec, so I gave him a call.

"JT!" Hec drawled when he answered. Hec's pronunciation of my nickname always threatened to turn it into a three-syllable phrase but never quite got there. "How the heck are you doing?"

I sighed, "Well, I'm still employed, and I have my health, so I'd have to say good, however possibly less than optimal."

"Uh oh, what's up?" Hec asked.

I recited my litany of woe with rising and falling frustration levels as I relived the particularly irritating events of my recent history. Unfortunately, I got so caught up in the venting that I over-shared a bit about my anxiety about being able to continue to provide for my mother.

When I'd finished my rant and paused to take a breath, I asked Hec, "Thoughts?"

Advice and an Offer

There was a moment or two of silence, then "Hmmm... Well, I've got comments from a couple of different perspectives."

"First, tactically, you are in a no-win situation with your manager. She's a surrender monkey. And you will always be looking over your shoulder as long as you work for her. Worse still, eventually, she will need to explain to her bosses why her group is under-performing, and she is going to need a scapegoat, and that scapegoat is probably going to be you. That alone is enough for me to suggest you make a move. But before you think about making a move, you need to consider my second comment, which is ..."

"Strategically, you need to be aware that pursuing a career in information engineering and data quality is going to be very different from other roles in I/T. If you are a great software developer, you are a rockstar in I/T, and people are thrilled when you show up. The results of your work are obvious and usually visible very quickly. If you are a good B/I Analyst, the fruits of your labor are readily apparent and eagerly consumed by executives at all levels. Executives smile when they see you in the cafeteria or run into you in the halls because you deliver tangible value."

"However, if you are an information quality advocate and you are pushing to collect solid quality data definitions before designing systems based on them, you are going to be perceived as a hindrance to speedy delivery."

"Encountering senior leadership that truly supports what is required to build an information-driven enterprise is extremely rare, to say the least. Unfortunately, leaders like Ranee Idler are not the norm."

"The executives that don't genuinely support information-centric activities are not necessarily bad people. They are just woefully ignorant in this particular area and are victims of a combination of factors that are a reality in our modern business environment."

"First, you get what you measure. There are very rarely any performance metrics or goals associated with information quality. Leadership measures I/T executives' success by tangible deliveries of software implementations, network uptime, infrastructure security, but rarely measure them on anything about data quality."

"The same is true of I/T projects. There are milestones associated with functional deliveries of software projects, but rarely any milestones or deliverables associated with data quality. Again, you get what you measure."

"Second, the difficulty associated with crafting business definitions makes development teams tend to try to avoid working through definitions so they can start coding faster. Most I/T folks didn't go into I/T because they liked writing prose."

"Third, the assumption that key terms are universally understood the same way is a powerful misconception. Pick the most fundamental concept you can, like product, or customer and ask a group of developers and business people to define it. In all likelihood, you'll be greeted initially with snorts of derision at how silly and obvious the task is. But if you stay with it, the odds are excellent that one part of the business will view (and define) "customer" differently than another part of the business. It is these semantic discrepancies, manifested in software and data as "bugs" which are extremely expensive and difficult to remedy with a universe of processes and code built on top of them."

"And finally, it is important to realize that working in information quality there is never an end to the work. You don't develop the perfect canonical data store, establish perfect governance around it, declare victory and move on because the natural forces of entropy are

ALWAYS attacking any progress you make. There will always be a development team that doesn't want to follow standards. There will always be an executive that thinks that their pet project is important enough to warrant an exception. So you must constantly be vigilant to defend the quality of the data and by extension the quality of the information."

"I say all of this to advise you that a far less stressful path will be in the area of software development and technology. You need to be truly fascinated with information engineering and information quality to go down that path because it is a lonely and stressful road, and your love of it will be the only thing that will keep you going sometimes."

"All that said, I've got more demand for information engineering resources right now than I can fulfill, so if you'd like to work with me, we can discuss that, too."

I was floored. I hadn't considered that, but the idea was intriguing. "Can I think about it and get back to you?" I asked.

"Sure! You should consider moves like this very carefully. You can't just pick up and move every time things don't go your way, but you must face reality at some point. I think that the variety of projects I've got going will provide you with a great opportunity to grow if information engineering is the regrettable career choice you make," he said with a somewhat wry tone.

"Would I be able to make as much consulting as I make in my current role?" I asked. "I've got to be sure I can support my mom."

"I'm fairly sure you'll make more. But, of course, how much more you make depends entirely on how busy you can stay to minimize the gaps between projects," Hec replied.

"You do need to manage your career a bit differently as a consultant too if you ever want to return to full-time employment with a company, but we can discuss that later if it becomes relevant," Hec concluded. "Just think about it and let me know."

We chatted a bit more about how things were going at Baker, how many bottles of water Lucy had knocked over, and I found myself drawn to be there and be engaged in really making a difference. I had some serious thinking to do.

The Last Straw

When I checked my email on Monday morning, I saw a note from MJ titled "See Me" with no additional explanatory text. I groaned inwardly because the chances were slim of that note meaning "See Me… I want to tell you what a spectacular job you are doing." So, with a sense of foreboding, I grabbed my notepad and a pen and headed for MJ's office.

I barely made it through the door before MJ started in with, "What is this email I'm getting from the business analysts where you are asking them to provide definitions for User, Customer, Profile, and Account?"

"Well, I was reviewing the use cases provided by the online ordering system development team as a start to building a conceptual information model for their domain and ran into these terms used interchangeably, so I was trying to get some clarity. I need definitions for those terms to know if they are synonymous, have supertype/subtype relationships, or possibly business relationships," I replied.

"Look," she barked, "I've worked on big systems before, and when we ran into things like this, we just made them one table, and it worked just fine. So don't be delaying the project teams with stuff like this anymore. Take your best guess at what it means and move on. We've got a lot of models to build. Now I've got a call to take, so please excuse me," she finished as she waved me toward the door.

I left her office and closed the door behind me, still in a bit of a daze. MJ had always been quick to surrender the high ground, but this was the first time she had just gone all out advocating for a dumpster-fire level of work-product. My best guess was that she was beginning to get pressure from above, and Hec's warning about who would be made scapegoat rang in my memory.

A quiet calm seemed to settle over me as I decided and headed back to my desk to type up my letter of resignation. Although still a little rattled from the conversation with MJ, the feeling of relief was palpable, and I was ready to take a new direction.

Resignation

I must admit that MJ's reaction to my presentation of my resignation letter the following day caught me entirely off guard. Based on the tone she had been using with me for the last couple of weeks and the fact that she had overruled me on every major decision for the previous month, I assumed that I was a thorn in her side that she would gladly jettison at the first opportunity. And while I still held that opinion, her feigned reaction was precisely the opposite.

"I must say JT that this is quite a surprise to me! You are a key member of the team, and we rely heavily on your contributions; you are leaving us in a lurch here by springing this on us!" she began.

When I didn't respond, she continued. "We've made some large commitments to deliver some profound changes around here, and I'm getting some very pointed questions about how we are progressing." She paused, obviously expecting me to say something. When I didn't, she asked, "Is this a big promotion? What is the company? Are you open to entertaining a counter-offer?"

"No," was all I replied.

"Well, I really think you are making a big mistake here. You had a bright future with Mycroft..." she began.

"...in a hospital ward recovering from a stress-induced stroke ...," I thought but kept my mouth shut.

"...but if your mind is made up, please provide as much transition support to the rest of the team over the next two weeks as you can. We are really sorry to see you go, JT," she said as she rose and extended her hand with her best pageant smile frozen on her face.

There were a dozen things that raced through my brain to say at that moment, but I just smiled, shook her hand, and said, "Thanks, I'll make sure the team has everything I've collected so far." and turned and went back to my workstation.

A couple of days later, the rumors started to filter back to me through the grapevine. MJ had indeed set up the story about our team's delivery struggles around the premise that I could not handle the workload and was falling behind in my commitments. So I made a note to buy Hec one of his favorite cigars as a thank you for giving me a heads up.

The Other Shoe

It was early on the Tuesday morning of my last week at Mycroft when one of the Senior Directors, Alec Hamm, with whom I had worked on various projects, dropped by my workspace.

"So," he began, "I hear you are leaving us."

"Yup," I replied, "My fun-meter was on 11, and I decided it was time to let someone else enjoy the ride for a while."

He smiled ruefully, "I hear ya'... Well, I just wanted to let you know that I'll be the one to conduct your exit interview at the end of the week."

When I looked quizzical, he said, "Technically, I'm your new boss."

As my eyebrows climbed to new heights, he smiled and said, "MJ has moved to a special project in administrative support."

"Huh," I said, letting the news soak in.

"I know this is a bit late to bring up," Alec continued, "but is there any chance that we could entice you to stick around and help move this forward?"

I thought for a second and replied, "I don't think so, Alec. I'm afraid that we've lost so much momentum and credibility across the organization at this point that it will be nearly impossible to resurrect the NextGen Data team as a credible force for change. There are just too many competing agendas and priorities driven by too many people positioned too high up in the business for us to affect any meaningful change around here."

Alec nodded as he listened and said, "I can understand how it looks to you, given what you've experienced; I just wanted to ask. I do plan on driving the effort forward, but it would just have been easier with experienced resources in place."

"I didn't make this choice lightly, Alec...," I began.

"I know, and I don't blame you; I just wanted to check and see if there was a way to salvage this." He replied.

"I'll be pulling for you," I said, "And if there's anything I can do over the next few days to help out, please let me know."

"Will do," he replied as he rose to leave, "And best of luck at your next engagement."

"Thanks," I said as I rose and shook his hand.

When we met for the debrief on Friday, I was honest and thorough with Alec. I reiterated the critical importance of getting clear, precise, and complete business definitions and documenting as many business relationships between the data elements as possible, preferably in some form of a model that could graphically represent the dependencies.

I outlined all of the attempts to start getting the definitions and how the various project teams and their leadership had thwarted our efforts.

I finished by advising him to keep trying to get executive-level support for the activity because it was crucial to have leadership support if these things were ever going to gain traction.

He nodded in agreement as I talked, not so much in commitment to pursue the recommendations I'd made as out of courtesy to me for having taken the time to share the thoughts.

When we finished, I shook his hand and started walking to my car.

As I walked through the building, down the stairs through the open dining area where I had spent so many hours discussing work and life in general with my co-workers, I was a bit nostalgic. Finally, I stopped at the guard station by the employees' entrance, turned in my badge, and said goodbye to Jake, the retired Marine with a big smile that was always a happy presence to start my day. He told me he was sorry to see me go, but then he winked and said with a smile, "Better things ahead, eh!?". I smiled and said, "I think so, Jake, I think so. Cheers!"

As I crossed the parking lot for the last time, I was sad leaving the place into which I had invested so much of my energy and the friends I had made along the way, but I was excited at the prospect of new challenges and learning new things.

The Baker of Baker Street Success

I showed up at Baker bright and early on Monday morning and was greeted at the security desk by Lucy.

"Hi!" she greeted me with a big smile, and I was a bit surprised at just how happy I was that she was the person that would be walking me in. There was something a bit different about Lucy this time, though. She spoke and moved with more confidence, and she was less likely to look away or change the subject. Hec had told me that she was growing into her new role, and she definitely had made significant strides in her confidence ..., and had her eyes always been that striking shade of blue?

I stumbled over the threshold as we entered the secured area, jostling me out of my musings. Thankfully, I caught myself just in time to hear Lucy say, "I'll take you to the project room so you can drop off your bag, and we can grab some coffee before we start digging into the project plan and getting you started."

The Project Room

As we entered the project room, I was momentarily taken aback at the charts and diagrams papering the walls. The room itself was of a size that could comfortably accommodate 12 people around a large conference table, with room for desks along the walls. However, instead of desks along the walls, a clear path starting at the door extended around the room. By following it, one could walk along a timeline presenting the proposed evolution of the company's information and data handling capabilities.

The diagrams and artifacts representing our "current state" starting point were to the left of the door. This presentation took up a sizable portion of the first wall because the team had pinned documents everywhere, encircling a highly summarized contextual model of the subject areas and broad business dependencies between them.

As one turned right on the path around the room, the second wall section was labeled "Federation." It contained more architectural diagrams outlining identifier matching strategies and targeted systems and data elements for the first shift toward integration.

In addition to these artifacts, there was a project timeline with upcoming projects and corresponding definition collection and conceptual modeling activities scheduled in advance of the formal project kickoffs.

One more right turn and the visitor faced the "Information-Driven Enterprise" wall with various images representing smiling executives, happy data scientists, Internet of Things devices, abstracted images of accounting ledgers, etc.

I had just taken in the last wall when a familiar voice behind me said, "JT! Welcome to the circus!" and I turned to see Hec's smiling face.

He shook my hand warmly and said, "We can walk through the layout of the room and the rationale later on this afternoon after you get settled. I see Lucy has you started, and she'll make sure you get all set up. But, right now, I have to rush off to meet with Ms. Idler to discuss some insurrection among the I/T folks and how we will deal with it," he said, bouncing his eyebrows up and down comically.

"Sure," I replied as he retreated out the door, and Lucy guided me to the conference table.

"We're using this as our base of operations," she said. "It has really helped us coordinate our efforts, and having so much of our reference materials readily visible on the walls has turned out to be a productivity booster."

"This is quite a setup!" I said, "How did you manage it?"

"Well, Hec had used something like it at a previous client to help communicate the vision to the Executive Leadership team. He'll do a better job of explaining the details this afternoon, but basically, he went to Ms. Idler and explained what he wanted to do, and she made the room available," Lucy replied. "It has been convenient to have a meeting room readily available whenever we needed it too! Juggling schedules and meeting rooms can be a pretty big pain."

We settled in and got my log in working and identified the software tools, accounts, and permissions that I'd need to get added, and then Lucy gave me a summary of what had been happening since my first visit.

Business Process Optimization By-Products

It was exciting to learn that our previous work around getting a clear definition for the concept of "Sales Order" had paid off tremendous dividends. The newly designed Wide Area Technical Sales Operations Network was now capturing orders so effectively that Baker finally hit the expected 24-hour delivery target.

In addition to the incremental benefits to the order entry application, once we had widely socialized the newly agreed-upon definition for Order, we discovered other optimizations in the business processes leading to even greater efficiency.

Insurrection

It turned out that the "insurrection" to which Hec had referred earlier was a related by-product of the new business process discussions that the standard definition of sales order had enabled. It was led by Cathy Summers and associated with a high-priority application development project requested by the CFO, Peter Jones.

Hec met with Ms. Idler to understand the situation, and they decided to schedule a more in-depth discussion later in the afternoon that same day.

When Hec returned to the project room, he was smiling broadly, and he didn't waste any time filling us in on what was going on.

"So, apparently, Peter Jones was so impressed with the speed of the newly optimized order entry application that he wanted to get that same kind of speed enabled for processing the credit card payments. Not only does he want it automated, but in a conversation with Jacob Parvender, the Director of I/T, it somehow was decided that it should be doable in six weeks. When they told Cathy Summers about it, she almost quit on the spot and then immediately began demanding an exception to going through the formal information requirements process."

Hec continued with a twinkle in his eye, "Imagine how she is going to react when I not only counsel against skipping the formal information requirements process but suggest that we spend the first three of the six weeks on information requirements! It should be entertaining, to say the least."

Hec chuckled as he continued, "I'm serious about thinking that we should spend half the time on information requirements, but if I have to back up to two weeks, I think that we can still capture enough of what we need to move forward effectively."

"I'm going to try to soothe things a bit by saying that we'll do the information requirements analysis and that they can work on tooling and non-functional and non-data-related coding during those first weeks. Hopefully, that will buy us some leeway with Cathy. I don't want her developers attempting to do information requirements gathering via random conversations anyway. Hopefully, she'll see the difference and value when she sees the output from a team of trained information requirements analysts. I believe that not only will we make up for any 'lost' development time, but that we'll speed up the final delivery by catching a whole host of bugs before they become code in the system and have to be rooted out."

Negotiations

The meeting went pretty much as Hec had predicted, with him asking for three weeks of information requirements, Cathy Summers exploding, and Hec letting her vent for 15 minutes until she got it all out of her system. Then Hec slowly started giving concessions.

First, he let them begin tooling and infrastructure (non-data-related) work in the first two weeks while we worked on information requirements.

Next, Hec promised not to ask developers to do any of the information requirements work. In exchange, he added chunks of time into the information requirements phase as he took tasks off the developers.

By the time they finished, he had gotten the two weeks that he had expected to. He had even gotten an acknowledgment from Cathy that the team might discover data changes after they began their sprints in earnest. Moreover, she committed to cooperating in accommodating those changes.

Facilitation

It was fascinating to watch Hec in these meetings, and one thing that I picked up on was his finely tuned ear for weasel words and intangibles. Repeatedly, he'd ask for clarification "What do you mean by <phrase>?" or "Now, help me understand," the latter being a masterful way of disagreeing with someone's idea/proposition without directly saying, "That's total nonsense."

If "Help me understand" was delivered with the proper tone, the other party was usually more than happy to help enlighten poor Hec to the brilliance of the idea that he was obviously missing. Often, in these situations, by the time the other party had finished "explaining" the concept to Hec and answering Hec's follow-up questions, they'd begun to see the point Hec was making. As a result, they typically either modified their position to a more reasonable one or completely abandoned it altogether when the ramifications were made apparent.

In the unfortunate circumstances where the other party refused to yield but had not made a compelling case for their position, further negotiations were made possible by keeping lines of communication open.

Accountability

Hec's premise of "doing what is right for the company" helped keep discussions calm for the most part, and differences usually boiled down to short-term tactical gratification versus long-term strategic positioning. When a strong enough case was for the tactical approach, the technical debt was acknowledged, itemized to the extent possible, and signed off on by all involved.

Cathy Summers was not a big fan of the sign-off requirement and tried to get out of it multiple times, but Hec was steadfast, and the risk of having the issue escalated was sufficient to get Ms. Summers to play by the rules.

By the end of the two weeks, Hec was satisfied. We used interviews with the business SMEs, analysis of existing paper and electronic artifacts, and web research followed by validation by the business SMEs to create our conceptual information model. As a result, we were confident we had a set of information requirements as complete as we could make them. They included data definitions defining our rudimentary conceptual information model that reflected what the business needed to know and what functionality the new electronic payment process would provide.

When we handed off the information requirements to the Dev team, they seemed pleased at what we provided and roared out of the gate, delivering a nicely functional proof-of-concept at the end of week three.

It was a pleasant surprise to hear the local and offshore developers comment on how handy the data dictionary had been and how much faster it had made the development go. They commented specifically on the reduction in instances where they ran into a question about a data element and were delayed waiting for clarification. Even Cathy acknowledged that it had been beneficial, and I chalked that up as a big win.

The Dev team showed why they were regarded so highly in the organization as they swiftly made modifications based on feedback and delivered a functioning solution right on time.

Actually, they had produced a solution by the end of week five that would have satisfied the original 'ask' but were able to entertain a couple of enhancements to the application in week six that took it from merely functional to being a joy to use.

When Hec, Lucy, and I met in the project room to discuss it, Hec said, "It was great to deliver what the company needed functionally in this application. But the thing that excites me even more is the change in Cathy's attitude about the information requirements process that began to become apparent as we went along."

"I honestly think that she started to see the speed improvements in the development process that came from the clarity of the definitions, and I do believe that she has embraced the approach. Of course, time will tell if the lessons stick but right now, I think we've made progress."

"I want to make sure that the significance of that sign-off process is not lost on you as we go forward. People resist signing off on the exceptions documents because they don't want a paper trail if things go pear-shaped. But the only way we will ever get widespread acceptance of doing things with a long-term benefit as a priority is if they have to take responsibility for every problem they cause by short-sighted thinking. Technical debt must have an owner if we are ever going to control it. If it is just allowed to accumulate anonymously, it will grow unchecked. Hopefully, over time, the sign-off process will reduce the rate of accumulation and cause everyone to think more about the long-term information health of the enterprise. Of course, there are no guarantees, but it is one control that can hopefully move us in the right direction."

Who Let the DOGG Out?

My third day back at Baker provided me with my first opportunity to see how the Data Oversight and Governance Group [DOGG] had progressed during my absence.

Hec had overseen most of the organizational, procedural, and staffing issues. Lucy served as his interface to the organization, identifying key people to contact for various departments and following up on resource requests to ensure we received them on time.

When it came time for the actual meetings of the DOGG to occur, Hec chaired the first one, but during the introductions, announced that Lucy would be chairing the DOGG in the future and that he would be serving in an advisory capacity only. He had discussed the matter with Ms. Idler, and she was enthusiastically supportive. Hec strongly felt that for Baker to thrive as an information-driven organization, they needed to cultivate and nurture the expertise to advocate for the principles supporting information-driven capabilities. Mr. Parvender had been pleased to have someone from his organization in the leadership role. Since Lucy hadn't yet established herself as a critical path resource on any of the current projects due to her newness to the organization, the transition was relatively seamless.

Hec and Lucy had long discussions before the first meeting. She was thoroughly versed in the overall Vision, primary strategies to be pursued, and various tactics that might prove helpful. She was excited and a bit nervous before the second meeting, when she actually took the reins, but Hec was there as backup, and she did splendidly.

Lucy was voracious in her study. As Hec recounted the story, he chuckled as he recalled some of the profound issues that she ran across fairly early in her evolution as an information engineer.

"Lucy was working with the Customer Relationship Management [CRM] team as they were trying to model their information requirements. Someone had done a bit of web research and had found a Party/Role model pattern from which they were borrowing bits and pieces. She was confused because one of the data architects had brought a model to the DOGG for feedback. They had modeled Customer as a subtype of Party. The justification was that the "is a" check indicated that this was how to model it. But they were getting all wrapped around the axle because they needed to be able to handle the fact that Parties could stop being Customers, and their solution didn't seem right to her, but she didn't know how to address it." Hec paused to smile. "I've known data architects that went YEARS without asking that question and even more that don't even know to ask it."

I looked at him a bit sheepishly and said, "Well, honestly, now that you mention it ...."

Hec grinned and said, "It is a bit confusing the first time you run across it, so remember the feeling because you'll be in the situation to explain it in the future to new data obsessives, and you may need to be patient while the pattern soaks in."

"The 'is a' heuristic, or 'rule-of-thumb' is just that, a clue, not a rule, and this is an example of an exception to that heuristic. So, for example, 'Customer is a Party' may be true at a given time. But, still, any time a statement can have a beginning or an ending date and time associated with it, that is an indication that you are talking about a Role rather than a subtype. So, if a Party may become a Customer and then stop being a Customer, you know the relationship is a role."

"On the other hand, if the 'is a' statement is persistent over time, you have stronger evidence of a subtype. For example, an Automobile will always be a Vehicle, so that is indicative of a subtype relationship."

"It may be a subtle distinction, but it can have significant impacts on the design once you take the requirement from the conceptual model and try to translate it into a logical design."

"Lucy's Laws"

One of the more interesting and unexpected developments as Lucy's time as leader of the DOGG progressed was how she had blossomed as a thought leader.

Hec had shared with us both a class book labeled: "Information Modeling for Information Engineers" he'd gotten almost 30 years ago in a class presented by someone named "Gary Schuldt." Gary proposed a collection of heuristics (or "rules of thumb" / guidelines) to derive an information model from plain business language. Lucy discovered a subset of these heuristics that she used more often than others in working with them. So she had started writing down a list of principles derived from the things that Gary had taught that she called "Lucy's Laws" with a twinkle in her eye.

Lucy's Laws centered around the rapid discovery of information requirements from reviewing available system artifacts and conducting interviews with the SMEs. Applying the repeatable information modeling patterns using well-defined data heuristics moved the creation of the data requirements from art to engineering because there were identifiable rational principles for the placement of every attribute and the structure of the ontology as a whole.

Lucy didn't make a big deal of it because that was just how her brain worked, but I could tell that Hec was pleased. He began calling out applications of Lucy's Laws every time we encountered one, and over time it became a game.

Lucy's Law #1 focused on discovering conceptual entities of interest to the organization by picking out the things that had attributes bearing their names.

Lucy's Law #2 focused on identifiers and codes used to identify something. If it has an identifier or code, it is probably an entity.

As excitement grew around formalizing the process, it became a game to see who could find a new law to add to Lucy's list.

Soon we had laws about entities, attributes, relationships, and subtypes and roles. The discussions in the DOGG model reviews became more and more orderly as the issues were couched more and more in principle and less and less in subjective opinion.

While opinion still had a prominent place in the discussions, we had reduced the number of entirely subjective arguments.

Wrapping up

About six months after my return to Baker, we were approaching the end of Hec's contracted initial consult with Baker and were wrapping up our involvement in the projects and processes.

The lifecycle process for new software, both in-house development and purchases and implementations of commercial off-the-shelf [COTS] packages, was very clearly defined and socialized widely across the organization. As would be expected, there were always instances of someone thinking that their new idea was either too business-critical or trivial in scope to justify going through the process. Still, Lucy and DOGG were relentless in hunting them down, so compliance remained high.

Despite occasional grumbling, the executives were already noticing the ease with which they could get new insights into their data and the reduced number of problems and rework they were encountering on software projects.

There was a wiki platform with company-wide access that now housed the corporate business language glossary. Anyone could enter new terms and edit old terms. Still, the DOGG had final edit/approval on all additions and changes and was doing an admirable job of ensuring that definitions were detailed enough and accurate according to how the Baker business culture used the terms.

Once it was up and running, the Baker glossary had been such a big hit that terms and acronyms flooded in at such a pace that the DOGG allocated a full-time resource to it for the first six months or so. After the initial surge, things slowed down to a pace that the DOGGies could divide the glossary up and manage it as a team.

It turned out that one of the most popular usages for the glossary was the cataloging and definition of acronyms and initialisms that permeated both the I/T and business cultures. As the collection became more and more robust and word of its value spread, it turned into the go-to place for acronym expansion. It was eventually added as a link on the internal corporate homepage and consistently ranked in the top five for click-thru.

As Hec had predicted, the improvement in their definitions of their key terms and specifically their data element definitions had resulted in a rapid expansion of their Conceptual Information Model. The precision of the data definitions had allowed some profound insights into their business relationships between critical entities. It allowed them to construct a model used as a roadmap to the information requirements of several new systems under consideration. The DOGG functioned as a requirement round-table where all the projects could discuss projects on which they were working. Quite a few conflicts had been identified early and avoided via enhanced communication.

As Hec and I discussed the happy results, his face grew grave, and he said, "You want to know how it all falls apart?"

I was a bit taken aback by this negativity, but I said, "Sure! Gloomy Gus, tell me, how does it fall apart?"

Hec smiled a wry smile and dipped his head, acknowledging my shot, and said, "Eventually, Lucy is going to gain enough seniority and experience to justify her moving up. Right now, she is the glue that is holding that whole DOGG together. All the DOGGies are gaining experience and are functioning as good team members. But it is Lucy's perspective, focus, passion, and spark that keeps it moving in the right direction. Imagine what will happen if Baker is not extremely serious in succession planning and lets that day she moves up or moves on sneak up on them. In that case, a hastily chosen replacement will have about a 2% chance of continuing their current progress effectively."

"Entropy is a powerful force of nature. Left unguided by a strong, knowledgeable, and passionate hand, the DOGG will atrophy into insignificance in a year or less. Moreover, when executives or developers try end-runs around the governance process, if the reasons for denying them are merely recitals of rules without reasoned explanations, over time, they will become less and less effective."

"However, we will include this admonition in our final report, so the hope is that Ms. Idler is persuaded and takes appropriate steps."

A Surprise

About that time, Lucy came over to our table and said, "Hi! Mind if I join you?"

"Not at all!" Hec said, rising, "I need to get back up to a meeting anyway; I'll leave you two in charge of the table!" He glanced at me with a faint smile as he left. "What was that about?" I wondered.

Lucy seated herself across from me and the morning light made her blond hair almost sparkle. She had grown so much over the year of working with Hec. Less the excited, fresh-faced rookie and more a seasoned young professional. Her smooth transition into the leadership role with the DOGG had surprised everyone, but she handled it as though she expected it all along. Her inquisitive mind was kept fully engaged, and her questions were frequently sparks for long-running investigations and discoveries. I found myself really looking forward to these conversations and would truly miss them when we moved on to our next project.

Lucy seemed a little fidgety for some reason as she began, "So, I guess you guys will be moving on shortly, huh?"

"Yup, apparently we've been engaged by LeStrade Environmental to work on some of their research data to try and clean out some corruptions that have been introduced over the years by unscrupulous researchers attempting to justify research grants," I replied. "It should be pretty interesting; we'll be working with business SMEs, researchers, and forensic auditors to try and enable some real insights."

"Cool" was all she said in reply as she stared at her coffee cup with a furrowed brow as if considering her following words carefully.

Finally, she looked up and said, "Well, since you are no longer going to be working under contract with Baker and there wouldn't be any conflicts of interest, would you like to go grab a pizza sometime?"

I confess that this caught me a bit off-guard, and I must have stared blankly at her for a second because she said, "Of course I understand if you'd rather …."

I quickly interrupted and said, "Sure! I'd love to grab a pizza with you! Anytime it works with your schedule."

A slight trace of relief washed over her face, and she relaxed into a smile, "Excellent! Do you like anchovies?"

The horrified look on my face must have spoken volumes because she said, "Better still… I know just the place!"

As we rose to go back to work, I thought that leaving Baker wasn't going to be quite as big of a drag after all.

Lucy's foot caught on the leg of the chair as she stood, and she stumbled, but I grabbed her hand, and she smiled and laughed as we headed for the door.

DO IT

Danger: Paradox Ahead

The most challenging concept for most aspiring Information Engineers to get their head around (after grasping the difference between the Conceptual Information Model as a "requirements" specification and the Logical Data Model as a design specification and what that means) is the love of questions.

> **It is easier to judge a person's mental capacity by his questions than by his answers.**
>
> *- Le Duc de Levis, (d. 1830), Maxims*

FIGURE 22 - QUESTIONS REQUIRE INSIGHT

Identifying questions as early as possible is extremely valuable. Documenting bits of business knowledge that the project team members (SMEs, executives, etc.) may not have thoroughly thought out or understood will be the primary antidote for bugs in code. This question and answer process must happen before designing, coding, and releasing software to support the business.

FIGURE 23 - I LOVE QUESTIONS

Every question that an architect drives out, documents, and answers in the process of deriving precise semantic definitions for every data element in scope, is a bug avoided and a potential disaster averted. The cost of fixing missing, misunderstood, or incorrectly assumed requirements goes up exponentially the later the project team discovers the unknown in the software delivery process/lifecycle. Finding these gaps in requirements should bring shouts of joy from every team member, from the most junior team member to the most senior executive.

> **The scientist is not a person who gives the right answers, he's one who asks the right questions.**
> - *Claude Levi-Strauss, Le Cru et le cuit, 1964*

FIGURE 24 - RIGHT QUESTIONS

Why does this work?

It is crucial for the information engineer to keep in mind (and to remind the business SMEs) that the information model they are constructing is **the business's model**. This work aims to capture what the business needs to know and how they want to operate, not dictate the answers for them. Gary Schuldt used to say, "We are mirror builders," that is, we are creating a model to reflect the business knowledge that the business SMEs are providing. It was telling that Gary would stop any information requirements meeting when the SME would say something like "Well, in your model..." to which Gary would reply, "No... this is YOUR model..." emphasizing the business's ownership of the model.

The fundamental premise of the approach to modeling information requirements under consideration here is that human beings communicate with each other using language constructs (grammar) that can be analyzed and translated into architectural constructs (a "Conceptual Information Model" [CIM]).

However, for this process to work, architects must ensure that every term used to describe the business is rigorously defined to eliminate synonyms and ambiguities.

Once the anchor points (entities) are clearly defined, the architect can identify and document business relationships between them that need to be supported.

While expanding the target audience for the data, modern systems and future systems will still need to map the data they are storing to specific ideas they represent. The Conceptual Information Model is the resource that can describe what is required to be known.

There is a dangerous assumption among many I/T resources that have worked in a particular business domain for a period that they do not need to engage the business for information requirements because they know the business "just as well" as the business resources. There are a couple of issues with this:

1) It is improbable that anyone thinking about a given subject (business domain) part-time or as a tangential activity to their primary responsibility will have an equal level of expertise with someone working in that business domain full-time. Moreover, the pace with which business strategies and regulatory requirements evolve in most business domains requires full-time involvement and dedication to stay current.

2) The creation of data stores and implementing systems to manipulate the data set business policy. If I/T does not consult and engage the business, I/T presumes to set business policy. If the computer systems provided by I/T do not support any aspect of the business, the company will have an exceedingly tricky time fulfilling that need. Therefore, it is vital to have businesspeople involved in the information requirements and provide guidance about how the business chooses to operate. The ideal situation would be to have someone from the business engaged that is authorized to set policy, but, likely, that level of resource will probably send a surrogate. In any event, sign-off and, therefore, ownership of the implemented business capabilities must rest in the hands of the business.

Shifting Gears from Data to Information

Author's Note

The approach described from this point forward for architecting information requirements is an accommodation to neophytes dealing with transitioning from technology-driven thinking to conceptual information thinking.

The terminology used is that of relational theory because it has a long history, a broad user-base, and the hope is that the familiarity of the terminology will help get the basic ideas communicated. The goal here is to provide a bridge into conceptual thinking and to get you started.

See my note at the end of the book for where to go next after mastering the basics.

A surprisingly significant challenge in transitioning to an information engineer / Conceptual Information Architect for most professionals with an I/T background is shaking off design-based (logical design) thinking. As pointed out repeatedly, the Conceptual Information Model is technology agnostic. The only constraint is that it directly reflects the business information requirement as communicated by the business without being influenced by current technology limitations.

FIGURE 25 - ARCHITECT REQUIREMENTS; DON'T DESIGN SOLUTIONS

Here are some symptoms of residual design-thinking:

1. Discussing "foreign keys."
   Foreign keys are a logical-level construct. Thus, the only thing that a conceptual model needs to document is the relationship, its name, cardinality, and optionality.

2. Obsessing over the highly normalized nature of the information model.
   "This can't perform; There are too many joins!" The information requirement is what it is. Design optimizations happen in the logical design model, and the preferred technology drives them. It would be ideal if the logical model could maintain a 1:1 mapping to the Conceptual Information Model, but what absolutely must not happen is changing the CIM to accommodate technological constraints. The responsible approach is to obtain specific maximum acceptable response-time thresholds from the SMEs, create the first-cut Logical Data Model (LDM) with a 1:1 map to the CIM, then run performance testing on that design to detect any response time challenges. If the LDM performs against the specified thresholds, leave the design alone because the flexibility provided by the normalization will pay off across the other transactions using the data structures in question.

   The purpose of the CIM is to inform multiple technologies, including future as-yet-unspecified technologies, so "tuning" it for specific current transactions and technologies inevitably "de-tunes" the structure for other transactions and possibly for future use as well, and defeats the purpose of the CIM as an integration hub.

3. Terse Entity/Attribute Names
   The priority of the CIM is to communicate the nature of the content of a data element effectively and efficiently with as little effort as possible. If the name of a data element can convey a precise understanding of the element's content without forcing the user to resort to looking up the description, it should. A solid business-language description is essential but should be considered a "backup" to a well-crafted element name.

Information Elements

Note In working through the information elements, it became tiresome to keep fully qualifying "Conceptual Entity," "Conceptual Attribute," "Conceptual Relationship," "Conceptual Role," etc.... and it is safe to assume that the reader would tire of it as well. Therefore, unless qualified otherwise, the elements under consideration may be assumed to be the "Conceptual" variation.

Many of us learned to "diagram" sentences as a part of our instruction in English in elementary school. We learned about nouns, verbs, subjects, objects, predicates, etc. and all of that translates directly into the activities covered here. For example, nouns represent candidate entities and attributes, and verbs can indicate candidate relationships.

Names

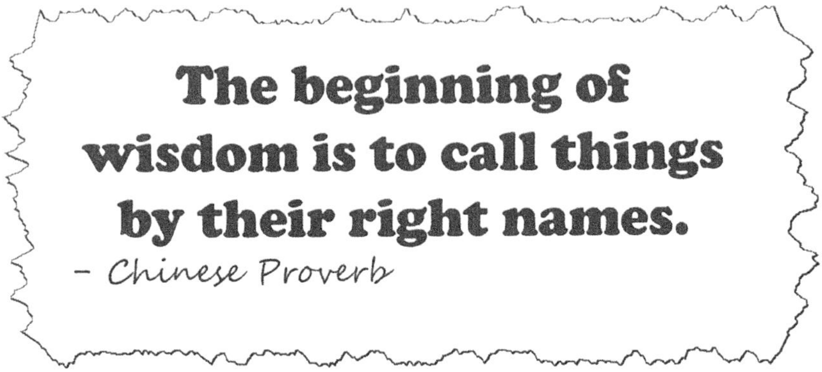

FIGURE 26 - RIGHT NAMES

Conceptual Information Model [CIM] names should fully describe the intended information content of the given data element. The designers at the logical level have complete autonomy in assigning logical names for the logical data elements, and the mapping back to the CIM should provide a last-resort source for clarifying the content.

Pro-tip Do not rush to fully qualify the names of elements or stress if you get hung up. Often this is because the fully descriptive definition of the element is not complete. However, once that definition is available, the proper name for the element becomes much easier to craft.

Names of entities and attributes need to:

- Use plain business language
- Be precise (no synonyms and no ambiguities)
- Be as long as necessary to describe the contents fully
- Not include technological or product names

Conceptual Entities

Entities should be named to represent clearly and specifically what they are. It is crucial to avoid brief names as they are typically too ambiguous, and more specificity is often required to describe the element's content fully. Premature finalization of the entity's name is probably counter-productive because as attribution evolves, the complete understanding of the nature of the entity's content may change. When that happens, it is essential to update both the entity semantic description and name as well.

Entities represent collections of Attributes that describe a given object, process, or state.

As demonstrated in Baker's sales order example, precise descriptions and names are vital to ensure that the Entities are correctly understood and handled at each processing phase in their lifecycle. The detailed information requirements for a "Tentative Agreement" may be vastly different than those for a "Finalized Order," and making a clear distinction between the two will ensure better content and more efficient discussions around business processes as well.

Conceptual Entity Discovery Toolbox

Lucy's Law #1 - *It has a name*

"Thou shalt consider any element with the word 'name' as a part of its own name as an indication of the existence of an entity." Any time a data element or attribute is labeled <YahdeeYahdee>Name, it is safe to say that <YahdeeYahdee> is probably some form of entity. E.g., CustomerName, VendorName, CardHolderName, etc. As in the examples provided, the actual nature of the entity may evolve into some form of subtype or role as the investigation continues. It is useful to document the probable existence of <YahdeeYahdee> for further elaboration.

Lucy's Law #2 - *It has an identifier*

"Thou shalt consider any element with an identifier for entity-hood." Attributes with names containing "...Code", "...Number", "...Id," etc., indicating that they are used to refer to something, are clues that the identified element should be treated as an entity and further elaborated. So <YahdeeYahdee>Code, <YahdeeYahdee>Number, and <YahdeeYahdee>Id would indicate, again, that there is an entity named <YahdeeYahdee> within the scope of the project that requires further investigation and definition.

Lucy's Law #3 - *It has values collected to describe it*

"Thou shalt consider any element for entity-hood that has attributes that describe it." In the unusual situation that project artifacts provide fully qualified attribute or field names, their names can associate them with their single-best-home entity, role, or subtype. E.g., PurchaseOrderEntryDate, PurchaseOrderAmount, InvoiceAmount, ProductItemUnitPrice, etc.

Lucy's Law #4 - *nouns [attribute evolution]*

"Thou shalt model any element as an entity when in doubt." When in doubt, initially model nouns as entities. If a further investigation determines that the element is value-bearing, the description of the contents should provide the single-best home for it.

However, keep in mind that over time, attributes tend to evolve into entities as more and more information about the value is requested (e.g., date entered, valid-thru date, the person entering, value history, etc.)

These are just clues. Further investigation will lead to the expansion and restructure of the model based on the guidance from the SMEs. The model will grow and change as the SMEs provide more input about each attribute, its usage, and its evolution.

Conceptual Attributes

Attributes are data-bearing objects that describe entities. As mentioned, over time, attributes can evolve into entities themselves.

A conceptual attribute has a "single best home" entity. Just because a transaction includes an attribute does not indicate that the conceptual transactional entity should include the attribute. (e.g., "Customer Name" may appear in a "Purchase Order"; however that is not the home entity for it.) This concept is one of the most significant points of contention between Conceptual Information Architects and DBAs and developers. The (conceptual) information requirement informs the resulting (logical) designs, but the (logical) constraints of the target platforms cannot be allowed to influence the structure of the (conceptual) Information Model, which has to remain technology-agnostic to support future growth and subsequent technologies.

Conceptual Attribute Discovery Toolbox

Lucy's Law #5 - *It is value-bearing*

"Thou shalt model any value-bearing data element as an attribute." This one is straightforward. If a data element carries a single "value," it refers to an attribute.

Once again, it is essential to remember that attributes tend to evolve into entities over time.

Lucy's Law #6 - *It has an entity Name as a qualifying part of its name*

"Thou shalt consider modeling an attribute as a part of the entity used in its name." Related to Lucy's Law #3, this law is one of the best ways to identify an attribute's "single best home." The problem is that fully qualified attribute/field names are rare in practice because it takes a few more keystrokes and time to enter and reference them. Scandalously short names are typically due to most analysts, architects, and developers alike being in too big of a "hurry" to do all that typing.

Lucy's Law #7 - *No multi-valued attribute groups (MVAGs)*

"Thou shalt never model a single attribute that contains concatenated values." Each attribute should contain a single atomic bit of non-decomposable data. The architect must decompose compound data elements into discrete attributes.

Business Relationships

Relationships represent interactions (e.g., "A Customer places one or more Sales Order") and dependencies (e.g., "A SalesOrder must contain one or more Product Item," "A Product Item may be specified on one or more Sales Order") between entities. Over time business relationships can evolve into entities themselves (e.g., "Customer Sales Order is placed on Customer Sales Order Placement Date") as attributes providing further insight into the business relationship are identified and defined.

Lucy's Law #8 - Verb phrases between Entities

"Thou shalt consider using the verb phrases in sentences connecting two entities to name the relationship between the entities." For example, when the statement "Customer places Sales Order" is encountered, either in interviews or in some form of artifact, the architect can identify the relationship "places" from Customer to Sales Order and "is placed by" from Sales Order to Customer.

The following clarifying questions are then generally helpful regardless of the anchoring entities on either end:

1. Can a Customer ever place more than one Sales Order?
2. Can a Sales Order ever be placed by more than one Customer?
3. Does a Sales Order have to be placed for a Customer to exist?
4. Does a Customer have to exist for a Sales Order to be placed?

At this point, someone occasionally snorts and claims that we do not need to ask those questions because the answers are apparent. So, let us explore a bit.

Re: Question 1 - Customer ever placed more than one Sales Order?

If the business is selling large dollar items (construction projects) that span long periods, it may very well opt to treat each new Sales Order as creating a new Customer. That situation is not common, but again, the effort here is to build an information model that mirrors the specific way the business under consideration operates.

Re: Question 2 – Can a Sales Order ever be placed by more than one Customer?

If the answer is "no," the follow-up question would be, "Well, have you ever considered 'buying groups?" If the answer is "yes," then the resulting change to the information model can save thousands of hours of rework and heartache for the development teams and business.

Re: Question 3 – Does a Sales Order have to be placed for a Customer to exist?

This question hinges on how clearly and precisely the term "Customer" has been defined and governed across the enterprise. Customer is one of those critical terms that elicit hoots of derision when asked to be defined but which potentially inspires heated debate if the participants in the discussion come from a broad enough cross-section of the enterprise. For example, sales and Marketing may have a vastly different view of "Customer" than Finance. Once again, the goal of the information model is not to influence how the business runs, it aims to reflect how the business runs, and this process is invaluable in driving out assumptions and eliminating synonyms and ambiguities, which are death to efficient implementation, operation, and support.

Re: Question 4 – Does a Customer have to exist for a Sales Order to be placed?

Questions like this help anticipate problems that may arise in the processing logic of the application when placing the first Sales Order for a given Customer. While not necessarily a "data" problem per se, it can help anticipate the process flow and any special coding that may have to occur.

It is vital to ensure that every identified relationship is named to indicate what business rule it represents. However, situations do occur where the same two entities have more than one relationship between them. Therefore, it is essential to be able to tell what relationships are already in the model.

Also, it is helpful to document the verb phrase so that making a sentence with the two entities involved can make sense regardless of which entity is named first. (e.g., "Customer places/is placed by Sales Order")

Subtypes and Roles

There is often a bit of confusion about the distinction between Subtypes and Roles. Therefore, it is essential to ensure that architects use the proper concept to support full attribution over the entity's lifecycle.

A simple check is to see if the state of specialization ever ends or changes. If a specialized relationship can end or significantly change, then the relationship is probably a "role" (e.g., "Party is a Customer as of <date>")

If the specialization is persistent, then the relationship is probably a subtype. (e.g., "A Person is a Party.", "An Organization is a Party.")

Lucy's Law #9 - *The IZZA check - "is a"*

"Thou shalt investigate the possibility of a subtype relationship when the phrase 'is a' joins two entities." One of the techniques used to determine subtype relationships is the "is a" check. E.g., "An Automobile is a Vehicle," and it is straightforward in this example. However, in practice, sometimes it can get a bit confusing when one encounters statements like "A Customer is a Person" and "A Person is a Customer." The confusion is that neither statement is universally true, which creates the need to differentiate between subtypes and roles.

Lucy's Law #10 - *The sometimes IZZA check - persistence check*

"Thou shall model what would otherwise be a subtype relationship as a role if the relationship can begin or end." In the previous rule, "An Automobile is a Vehicle" is a persistent truth (ignoring the usage of Automobiles as pieces of art for a moment), just as a Vehicle does not necessarily have to be an Automobile.

For the "Customer is a Person" vs. "Person is a Customer" dilemma, neither statement is necessarily persistently true. A Customer may be an Organization, and a Person may become a Customer and then stop being considered a Customer based on how the business decides to track the relationship. The fact that a Customer may be an Organization or a Person points to the need to investigate abstracting Person and Organization into Party. The possibility of a transitory Customer relationship in the second example leads to the need to track start and stop dates for the relationship, implying a role-type relationship.

Assumptions

An aspect of information requirements that often gets overlooked is documenting explicit decisions by the business to leave things out of the model. When the architect only tracks what made it into the model, questions may arise later about why something is missing. For example, we often lose track of the underlying decision to omit an element/factor or the person's name authorizing the simplification in the flurry of discussions and decisions in fast-paced information requirements meetings.

Therefore, it is vital to model/track what makes it into the model and document decisions (assumptions) made to leave things out of the model.

Again, this model is the responsibility of the business. It is their model. It is vital to ensure that the business has engaged and made all decisions about the contents of the resulting architecture.

A project team can track assumptions in something as simple as a spreadsheet or a small desktop database. Assumptions need to include: Description of Assumption, Person Authorizing Business Decision, Date Assumption Captured, and Ramification Description (Why was the Assumption required and what may be any foreseeable consequences?).

Question-and-Answer Log

The project team should maintain a Question-and-Answer Log (Excel spreadsheet could suffice). The log should track the text of the question asked, when asked, who asked it, who the appropriate SME to ask should be, the text of the answer received, and when the answer was received. This tracking is critical to ensure that the questions get addressed and provide some guidance on who to follow up with for any further questions.

This analysis artifact is instrumental in reviewing business artifacts where an SME may not be immediately available to address the questions.

General Notes

"Clues" vs. "Absolutes"

FIGURE 27 - LOOKING FOR CLUES

It is important to note that the laws listed here are just starting points. They are not "absolutes." Instead, they offer a catalyst for further investigation by the architect.

For example, if an architect is conducting an interview or reviewing a document and encounters the phrase: "Customer Name," at least two of Lucy's Laws apply… "Lucy's Law #1 – It has a name" and "Lucy's Law #6 – It has a Conceptual Entity Name as a qualifying part of its name". Initially, the architect should model this as an entity named "Customer" with an attribute called "Customer Name." However, further investigation may reveal that "Customer" is a role and that the name may have a home on a super-type (possibly "Organization," "Person," or "Party"). But the architect should capture it following the laws first, and further clarification from the SMEs will drive the ultimate home for the attribute.

"Always" and "Never"

Listen for asserted absolutes and challenge them to avoid baking untested simplifying assumptions into the CIM. For example, any time the words "always" or "never" get dropped into a discussion of business requirements by an SME, a trained requirements analyst should be alerted to press further. E.g., "Purchase Orders are ALWAYS submitted by one Customer" ... What about Buying Groups? By listening and challenging, the analyst can avoid potential data mismatches with the business requirements. In addition, by prompting a moment of reflection, the business SME may discover new business opportunities, which are always an excellent "value add" to provide.

"Good" Definitions

Eliminate Ambiguities and Synonyms

One of the significant challenges in working with legacy siloed data structures is that the names provided were typically produced in a hurry as a "necessary evil" to get back to the process of coding as quickly as possible. Consequently, excessively terse element names, combined with missing or abbreviated descriptions for the data elements, result in synonyms and ambiguities in the environment.

For purposes of this discussion, a "synonym" is a data element whose intended content appears to be the same as another data element. An "ambiguity" exists when data representing two different meanings can be loaded into a single data element.

An example of a "synonym" would be an Entity named "Purchase Order Line Item" with two attributes named "Price" and "Amount." Better names would be "Product Item Unit Price" and "Purchase Order Line-Item Total Amount." Note that the names tend to indicate what the actual "home" conceptual entity should be when fully qualified.

An example of an "ambiguity" would be a Purchase Order entity with an Attribute named "Date." Without a constraining definition, this Attribute could be tracking "Purchase Order Entry Date," "Purchase Order Approval Date," "Purchase Order Cancellation Date," "Purchase Order Fulfillment Date," etc.

Are as lengthy as needed

In data element descriptions, the analyst must include all pertinent characteristics of a particular data element. Again, the primary goal is to clearly define the intended content while ruling out synonyms and ambiguities.

Always be selling the value of definitions

It is vital to keep communicating why investing the time, effort, and resources into good definitions is of value.

Solid definitions enable:

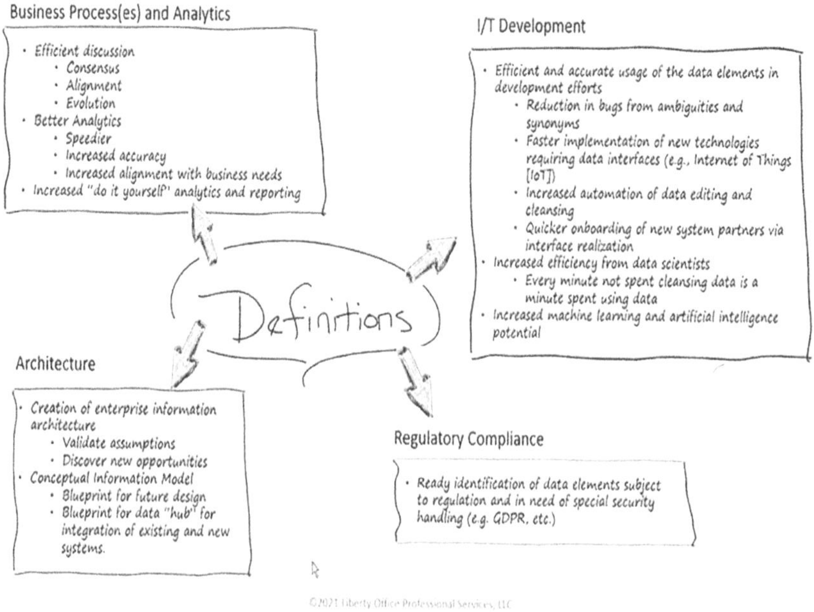

FIGURE 28 - BENEFITS OF DEFINITIONS

Progress Accelerators

Over nearly three decades of pursuing information excellence in multiple Fortune 500 clients, a few handy practices have revealed themselves. Of course, these are subjective so consider them advice from a friend. However, the hope is that you will benefit from some of the "scar tissue" that these recommendations represent.

Clearly define and ruthlessly defend scope

Information, in and of itself, has no natural "scope" or boundary. It is possible, indeed highly likely, that any time a project begins an information model for a given enterprise, project, or other initiatives, eventually interested parties will propose that you include adjacent or tangentially related subject areas. "While you are at it ..." It is critical to very clearly enumerate what subject areas are within the scope of a given effort. Still, it is equally critical to identify any known adjacent or tangential topics or subject areas and explicitly enumerate them in the initial definition of scope as "out of scope." The project team must require an adjustment to the proposed timeline for delivery if expanded subject areas get brought into scope.

Who cares?

There are almost infinite attributes that can be included in an information model. Just because something might be useful to know at some point does not justify expending the effort to define it and include it in an information model.

Consider the following questions:

1. Who cares enough about this attribute to populate it?
2. Who cares enough about this attribute to govern and maintain it?
3. What is the business benefit derived from having this attribute?
4. Is this attribute of interest to the enterprise generally, or is this attribute of a functionally-specific scope?

To illustrate this issue, Gary Schuldt used to say that "Inter-ocular Distance," when defined as "the distance between the center point of a given person's eyes," is an attribute that applies to all persons in the system. But unless the enterprise needs such a data point (e.g., developing facial recognition software), who will be motivated to capture this data and maintain it?

FIGURE 29 - NOT A STRAW MODEL 10

Start with a "straw" model

A helpful tactic to demonstrate respect for the limited amount of time that business experts have available to share is to research and develop as many industry-standard definitions for common business terms as possible. They can then be the basis for a "thought starter" data dictionary and Conceptual Information Model (CIM) that the SMEs can critique.

Review any business artifacts

The architect should mine any available document artifacts for candidate information elements. **Business glossaries** are typically gold mines for candidate data elements that can be structured, placed, and refined as the semantic descriptions evolve. Working through these and all subsequent artifacts will yield an assortment of follow-up questions to be routed to the business subject matter experts (SMEs) for clarification and elaboration. Identifying these questions and the answers provided before any design or coding work provides powerful "bug reducing" benefits. Without this work, assumptions are made and codified with expensive and time-consuming results.

Use cases and other process documentation can yield additional data elements and identify the connecting dependencies that represent relationships between the data elements.

Wireframes, screenshots, and existing system documentation can yield candidate information elements, but great care must be exercised to avoid letting technical considerations influence the information elements included. Additionally, these layouts can imply relationships between elements that can be investigated further and validated. Finally, as always, exhaustive, precise business language descriptions need to be obtained.

Consult any industry-standard glossaries

Industry glossaries are target-rich artifacts, but the analyst must ensure that the definitions provided precisely match how the enterprise uses the term. Differences should be explored in the Question-and-Answer Log and tracked.

The project team should emphasize the effort to streamline the definitions process to the business subject matter experts (SMEs). It is essential to reassure them that their time is valued. A vital part of selling enterprise information is ensuring that everyone is aware of the unacknowledged backroom work.

Be specific; Drive questions and reactions

If the project team must create "straw" definitions to start the conversation, they should intentionally word them as precisely and restrictively as possible. The goal is to elicit a response from the reviewing SME. Ambiguous descriptions leave too much room for error and frustrate efforts to use them as guidance in meticulously designing accurate data edits or effectively using the values in calculations or reporting. Thus, the value in getting SME guidance in tightening up the descriptions at this point is critical.

Track sourcing for descriptions

All definitions should have a "source" clearly identified for them. For example, if no industry-standard vocabulary exists and no enterprise definition is available, the Conceptual Information Architect must create one. In that case, the analyst must identify themselves as the author of the straw definition and solicit feedback. This approach usually gains enthusiastic feedback from SMEs. Because, while creating a new description from scratch is painfully dull for most SMEs, finding flaws in someone else's thinking seems to be great fun.

The upside is, once the definition is edited per the SME, that SME becomes the attributed source for the definition.

The goal is an enterprise SME as the attributed source for each definition in the scope of the effort. The purpose is not to blame but to provide an authoritative source for clarifications and demonstrate that this model represents the business's knowledge and not some assumption made by an architect. These descriptions limit how the business operates, and therefore a responsible and qualified SME must be the source.

Limit requirements meetings to business experts only

It bears repeating yet again. The Conceptual Information Model (CIM) should be a model of the pure business information requirements described in plain business language and entirely driven by the needs of the business. Experience has taught that any time I/T resources participate in these discussions, previous system implementations or technology constraints get injected into the discussion, which is a distraction and counter-productive to understanding what the business truly needs to know. Enterprise Data Warehouse (EDW) technicians loathe discussing information requirements that have no identified data source. While this is understandable in a warehouse design discussion, the goal in this effort is to discover potentially unfulfilled business information needs.

Ensure that all conceptual models use business language

To the extent possible, plain business language must be used in creating the Conceptual Information Model (CIM) that is readily understandable by all the business people in the company. This clarity of language will be invaluable to newly hired company personnel.

Each enterprise, and possibly each functional division, will probably evolve a shorthand dialect to expedite internal communication. However, a more disciplined vocabulary is required when discussing business concepts that span a broader context. Thesauri and descriptions can serve to bridge any gap.

Avoid acronyms, abbreviations, and initialisms

Avoiding acronyms, abbreviations, and initialisms helps achieve the goals of useability and enduring value. If necessary, spell out the full name and associate it with the appropriate acronym, abbreviation, or initialism the first time used. Unfortunately, all industries are rife with these as professionals try to short-cut communication and avoid tripping over long names in conversation and communication. However, in this context, clarity is the primary objective, and assumptions are the enemy.

Avoid system names, technology names, and brand names in descriptions

The primary reason to avoid system names, technology names, and brand names is that they are typically used to 'shortcut' a full explanation of the function they represent. The project team may discover potential unknowns and resolve them early by spelling out the underlying functional role.

Additionally, one of the critical benefits of the Conceptual Information Model is its potentially long useful life. Technologies come and go, but when thoughtfully constructed and maintained, the Conceptual Information Model will outlive all the technologies in use at the time of its initial construction.

Finally, as a "hub," it is vital that the descriptions talk about the functions in the language of the business to be able to serve as a point of common understanding across all consuming systems and through time.

Accommodating functional dialects

There is no need to have an "iron-fist" mandate across the enterprise that staff only use the canonical names derived in these efforts for day-to-day conversations and business activities. However, when a given piece of data is of use across the enterprise (or even more widely), a "standard" name and description applies (E.g., "Customer," "Sales Order," "Product," etc.). Further, communications with parties outside the functional area (i.e., the enterprise level) must use this canonical name.

Ensure business buy-in and participation commitment

It cannot be over-emphasized that the business is the owner of the data in the organization and, as such are primarily responsible for its quality. I/T has a logistical responsibility, but the business is ultimately responsible for the accuracy and cleanliness of the data content that it needs to function correctly.

To this end, knowledgeable businesspeople authorized to make decisions for the business must be active participants in the information requirements gathering and documentation efforts.

An active role ensures a better representation of the business's needs and achieves a "buy-in," which reduces "sniping from the sidelines" as capability reviews occur.

Establish Non-Functional Data Requirements

A correctly built Conceptual Information Model is going to be at least Third Normal Form (3NF), and the first instinct of developers and DBAs in laying out their subsequent design is going to be to "simplify the design," i.e., start "de-normalizing" the data. Since changing the database structure is the most expensive form of "tuning," prematurely allowing technical constraints to influence a design to favor particular transactions or use cases is a costly mistake. It is preferable to have a known performance target (e.g., "maximum response time") and then only tune until the transactional performance has achieved that target. There is no such thing as "intuitive design" when it comes to data. Database technologies and system speeds have increased at such a rapid pace that a structure that might not have performed rapidly enough five years ago might well deliver results within a specified response window. In any case, tuning should be done against specific criteria and stopped when performance meets those criteria.

Establish Key Data Quality Performance Indicators

Before undertaking any data quality enhancement effort, it is critical to get a quantifiable picture of the problem to measure the value of the work done to improve data quality. Of course, dollar figures are the best, but error counts per unit (transaction) processed are also helpful.

Final Note on "Do it"

This work has emphasized the importance of establishing clear communications upfront, persisting collected business requirements knowledge, and using Conceptual Information Modeling to shape the information requirements in a manner readily translated into designs across technologies and through time. We've presented some initial concepts and techniques we've found productive to get started, but we've avoided particular paradigms or syntax.

The concepts and tools presented here will deal with over ninety percent of the information modeling situations a working Conceptual Information Architect will encounter. However, as a next step for precisely and rigorously capturing information requirements, it is highly recommended that you refer to "Information Modeling and Relational Databases 2nd Edition" by Terry Halpin and Tony Morgan [11]. Dr. Halpin's Object Role Modeling [ORM] technique described in his book directly supports mapping human language to a technologically agnostic architecture capable of being implemented using any desired logical approach to data persistence.

ORM is the de facto standard of excellence for Conceptual Information Modeling. The elegance of treating named elements as objects allows them to reveal themselves for what they are as you learn more and more about how they inter-relate with the other objects within your universe of discourse.

I wish you well as you unravel your own mysteries and write your own stories.

GLOSSARY

BDUF [Big Design Up Front]

"...a software development approach in which the program's design is to be completed and perfected before that program's implementation is started." [12]

Canonical

In this context, the working definition of "Canonical" used intends to convey the idea of "approved," "authoritative," or "according to standard".[6]

Conceptual Level

A level of modeling that is more detailed than the Contextual level, allowing for the broader concepts outlined in the Contextual model to be elaborated to a sufficient level of detail to serve as guidance for subsequent solution designs and cross-reference mappings. It is detailed (to the attribute level), business-centric, and technology-agnostic. At this level, the focus is capturing the information requirements of the business in as rigorous a manner as possible to inform future design decisions and serve as a roadmap for business consumers looking for information.

Contextual Level

The Contextual level is a summary view of the information needs of the business at a broad subject area level. At this level, information relationships and dependencies serve as a roadmap for further elaboration by the Conceptual modeling efforts. In addition, this level is helpful for executive-level communications and obtaining buy-in and validation of alignment between executive leadership and the requirements gathering professionals.

Logical Level

The Logical Model level is the first level of "design" and is the first level where technological constraints apply. At this level, the focus shifts from information to how the data representing that information will be configured and persisted for reuse. At this level, the designer knows what paradigm for storage applies (e.g., Relational Database, Hierarchical Database, Flat File, Hadoop, etc.) and incorporates the technical constraints of the given paradigm in implementing the information requirements documented in the Conceptual information model as a Logical Model design.

Normalized

Normalization is the process of streamlining and stabilizing data structures first proposed by Edgar F. Codd in 1969. Architects generally consider a database "normalized" if taken to the Third Normal Form (3NF). In practice, the methods described here for settling attributes in their "single best home" go a long way toward achieving 3NF. A deep dive into normalization is beyond the scope of this effort, but Codd is the authority on it, and his works are highly recommended for those deeply interested in the topic.[7] [8]

Physical Level

The Physical level is the next level of technological constraints after the Logical model. This level is where the designer factors a given implementation (e.g., Oracle, DB2, Azure, etc.) of a paradigm's needs for storage into the design. Again, it is helpful to think of "brand names" coming to bear here as this level represents vendors' specific implementations of a given paradigm.

Subject Matter Expert (SME)

A person who has a deep understanding of how the business runs, constraints under which the business must operate, past assumptions about the business, and any future directions that the business would like to embrace.

Technology Agnostic

As used in this work, it refers to not being influenced by technological preferences or constraints.

Third Normal Form (3NF)

A working definition of 3NF is when the architect has placed every attribute in its "single best home."

However, for those that need a more challenging concept, there is this definition: *"A relation is in third normal form if there is no transitive dependency for non-prime attributes (and is also in the second form...)"*[9]

REFERENCES

1 Kallman, Ted and Andy. *Flow: Get Everyone Moving in the Right Direction …and Loving It*, New York, Morgan James Publishing, 2018

2 https://en.wikipedia.org/wiki/Technical_debt

3 https://hostingtribunal.com/blog/big-data-stats/

4 https://www.zachman.com/about-the-zachman-framework

5 https://businessoverbroadway.com/2019/02/19/how-do-data-professional s-spend-their-time-on-data-science-projects/

6 https://www.dictionary.com/browse/canonical

7 Codd, E.F (1969), Derivability, Redundancy, and Consistency of Relations Stored in Large Data Banks, Research Report, IBM.

8 https://web.archive.org/web/20070612235326/http://www.acm.org/classics/nov95/toc.html

9 https://www.techopedia.com/definition/22561/third-normal-form-3nf

10 Pearson Scott Foresman, Public domain, via Wikimedia Commons

11 Halpin, Terry and Morgan, Tony, Information Modeling and Relational Databases 2nd Edition, New York, Morgan Kaufmann Publishers, 2008

12 https://en.wikipedia.org/wiki/Big_Design_Up_Front

13 https://www.credit-suisse.com/about-us-news/en/articles/news-and-expertise/mark-cuban-data-is-the-new-gold-201706.html

Understandability – Each data element should be thoroughly and uniquely defined to ensure proper usage and interpretation.

Accuracy – Each data element should have processes to ensure that the values contained therein are correct and current.

Flexibility – Data structures should be built in such a way as to facilitate reuse across existing systems as well as being able to adapt to support future requirements rapidly.

Usefulness – Data collected and maintained should be suitable for and have value to a business usage by the enterprise.

Reliability – Data stores should be structured to ensure they remain available.

Accessibility – Data should be maintained in such a way that all interested parties can get to it.

Security – Data should be protected to ensure that only legitimate users can access it.

Comprehensiveness – Efforts should be made to ensure that all of the required data needed by the business is available.

Made in the USA
Monee, IL
04 November 2026

67387551R00108